JADES
FROM THE HEI-CHI COLLECTION

熙墀藏玉

姜涛　刘云辉　编著

文物出版社

2006 · 北京

封面设计　程星涛
装帧设计　郎　艳
责任印制　梁秋卉
责任编辑　张小舟

图书在版编目（CIP）数据

熙墀藏玉／姜涛，刘云辉编．—北京：文物出版社，
2006.3
ISBN 7-5010-1866-9

Ⅰ.熙…　Ⅱ.①姜…②刘…　Ⅲ.古玉器－中国－图录
Ⅳ.K876.82

中国版本图书馆 CIP 数据核字（2006）第 003515 号

熙墀藏玉

姜涛　刘云辉　编著

文物出版社出版发行
北京五四大街 29 号
http://www.wenwu.com
E-mail:wwyk@wenwu.com
北京圣彩虹制版印刷技术有限公司印制

889 × 1194　1/16　印张：14
2006 年 3 月第一版　2006 年 3 月第一次印刷
ISBN 7-5010-1866-9/K · 977　定价：260 元

目 录
Contents

自 序

熙墀

　　熙墀藏玉始源于上世纪六十年代末期，至今已三十余年。于此期间所得选藏传世玉器凡三百余件。论及时代，上则可溯至五千余年前的氏族之期；中可涵三代、两汉；下可达唐、宋、元、明、清。熙墀藏玉有别于博物馆藏品，除注意其历史、考古及文物价值外，尤其偏重于其整体艺术价值。故藏品中除片状玉雕外，较多为半圆雕及立体圆雕玉器，而其中多为肖生玉雕，此为熙墀藏玉中之一大特点。玉之为器，源远流长，人类文明起源之时，即有玉器现身。三代之前，巫术借此通天地达鬼神；三代之内，治国者凭此定礼制、区等级、别贵贱、礼天敬祖；三代之后，帝王之家、达官贵人、寻常百姓，同好此道。自古至今，他类文物此消彼长，唯独玉器从不间断，一部华夏文明史可于玉器中得窥其全貌，此乃熙墀选藏玉器重要因由之一也。

　　熙墀藏玉多年，素有一心愿，适时将其选编成册，留为纪念。年前已着手工作，于三百余件藏玉中选出较好之玉作，刊印成册，与同道共享。此事得成，则余心愿足矣。

　　熙墀藏玉多年，虽自觉已微有心得，但也深谙此道精深，特别是在玉器的断代与辨伪上，每每有功力不足之感，故此在收藏过程中常抱业余之心，旨在分享收藏之经验与快乐。深愿藉本册小书刊印之机会，求教于方家，还望专家学者、同道好友，多多包涵，不吝赐教，则不胜感激之至。

　　本书编撰过程中得到了多位专家、学者及同道好友的帮助与鼓励。特别是郭大顺先生、姜涛先生及刘云辉先生。是次选出的数件红山玉器，承蒙郭大顺先生赞谓传世品中难得一见之物。又蒙姜涛、刘云辉两位先生慨然允诺是次遴选玉器及协助整理，并编写目录条文。谨藉此机会向他们表示万分感谢。本册编辑过程中，承蒙香港洪树坚先生、胡宇明先生及何世礼先生费时两年，鼎力完成玉器摄影工作。又，本册部分玉器是由文物出版社孙之常先生及河南省文物考古研究所祝贺先生协助拍摄完成的。本册所有玉器的墨拓工作是蒙河南陈英女士相助完成的，精美的拓本使本书增色不少。本书所有的英文翻译工作是由香港中港考古研究室王文建先生相助完成的。他们的慷慨与热心促成了本册小书的完成与出版。本册小书的出版与发行，还得益于文物出版社的大力相助，他们的精心编排与辛勤劳作使本书增辉不少，藉此书付梓之际，谨向他们一并致深切谢意。

　　需要特别提出感谢的是，著名专家、学者李学勤先生为熙墀所藏商代刻铭玉璧专门赐下《释香港钟华培先生玉璧刻铭》大作一篇，释疑解惑，为本书增色不少。又，著名玉器专家杨伯达先生为此书的出版，专门写来贺词。在此，对二位一并表示深深的谢意。

　　再次对为本书编辑出版付出过辛劳的所有专家、学者及朋友们表示本人最深切的感谢。

乙酉年孟冬
于香港

AUTHOR'S PREFACE

Hei-Chi

It has been over 30 years since the late 1960s when I began to collect jades. During this period, I have selected and collected over three hundred pieces of jade. As for the dating of my collection, the earliest ones can be traced back to the clan-lineage society of over 5000 years ago; those in the middle range of time cover the Three-dynasties of the Xia, Shang and Zhou and two Han dynasties; the late ones are from the dynasties of the Tang, Song, Yuan, Ming and Qing. My collection is different from museum collections in that, in addition to paying attention to the historic, archaeological and relic values of the jades, I have especially emphasized the overall artistic value of my collection. Therefore, except for some flake shaped pieces like the *bi*-disk, the majority of my collection consists of semi-round figures and three-dimensional figures in the round. Among these figures, zoomorphic figures further outnumber other types, and best characterize my collection. The tradition of making jade into utensils is ancient in origin and enduring through history, and jade had already appeared at the start of human civilization. Before the Three-dynasties, *wu*-sorcery employed jade to communicate between Heaven and Earth to reach the spirits. During the Three-dynasties, the rulers of the states used jade to establish rites, to differentiate hierarchical ranks, to distinguish the high and the low, and to worship Heaven and ancestors. After the Three-dynasties, regardless of their status as the royal family, the noble and rich or the commoners, people have all been fond of jade. From ancient times to the present, other sorts of cultural relics have emerged and disappeared-only the jades have appeared incessantly. The history of the Hua-Xia civilization can be appreciated through the tradition of jade and this significance is one of the important reasons for me to collect jades.

I have been collecting jades for more than three decades, and it has always been my desire to publish the selected pieces at a suitable time to commemorate my effort. I initiated the work last year, selecting the most refined from over three hundred pieces in order to compile a book to share with people with the same interest. Now that this book is going to be published, my desire has been completely satisfied.

After collecting jades for so many years, I believe that I have acquired some knowledge. However, I am fully aware of the profoundness of the field and, especially when confronting the issues of dating and authenticity, my shallowness in knowledge. Therefore, I have always considered myself an amateur in the collecting process, and intend to share with others my experience and happiness during this process. I truly believe that the publication of this small book is an opportunity for me to learn from specialists, and I gratefully welcome critiques and teaching from all scholars and friends.

During the compiling of this book, I have received help and encouragement from many specialists, scholars and good friends with the same ideals, but especially from mainland scholars Mr. GUO Dashun, Mr. JIANG Tao and Mr. LIU Yunhui. It is an honor that the selected Hongshan jades in this book are praised by Mr. Guo as exceptional among the collected jades from the Hongshan culture. Mr. Jiang and Mr. Liu have kindly accepted my request to assist me in the process of selection and research and to write catalogue entries. I would like to use this opportunity to express my deep gratitude to them. During the process of editing this book, I have also had the help of Mr. Hung Shu-kin, Mr. Wu Yu-ming and Mr. Ho Sai-lai from Hong Kong who spent two years to accomplish the task of taking photographs. Mr. SUN Zhichang from Wenwu Press and Mr. ZHU He from the Henan Institute of Archaeology also helped photograph jades for this book. All the excellent rubbings in this book were performed by Ms. CHEN Ying from Henan Province. Her rubbings have added a great deal of luster to this book. All the work of English translation in this book is accomplished by Mr. WANG Wenjian from the Hong Kong Institute of Archaeology. It is the generosity and enthusiasm of those I mention above that helped to bring about the completion and publication of this book. The publication and distribution of this book also rely on the great support from Wenwu Press, where editors have greatly improved this book with their careful hard work. I would like to extend my deepest heartfelt gratitude to them at the time of publication.

I should particularly thank the renowned scholar, Prof. LI Xueqin, who wrote a great essay in which he deciphered the inscriptions on the Bi-disk of the Shang from my collection. Prof. Li's work is enlightening and greatly improves this book. Additionally, the famous scholar and jade specialist, Prof. YANG Boda, wrote a warmhearted essay to praise the publication of this book. I would like to thank both of them deep-heartedly at this time.

Lastly, let me again express my profound gratitude to all the specialists, scholars and friends who have taken pains to help complete and publish this book.

Hong Kong
Late winter, 2005

序

姜　涛

　　熙墀先生崇爱玉器，不仅鉴赏极精，而且入藏颇丰。今次先生从其所藏凡三数百件玉器之中，遴选出较好之玉作，刊印成册，与同道共飨，同世人齐观，展其貌于当前，存其容于后世，实乃收藏界之一大幸事也。此书一经刊出，于玉器的鉴赏与研究必多有益处。

　　观我华夏文明源远流长，博大精深。先哲和前人留给我们的文化遗产与遗物门类繁多，反映并折射出独特的华夏文化面貌，而其中之玉器更是引人注目。自古至今，它类文物此消彼长，唯有玉器伴我人类不眠不休，一部华夏文明史于玉器之中，得窥其全貌也。

　　先生今次所选的二百余件玉器，包含颇丰。从时代上看，史前、商周、两汉及唐、宋、元、明、清均有涉及。从地域上看，则北可至白山黑水、松辽平原；南可达长江两岸、江浙苏杭；东可至东方沿海；西可达黄土高坡。从其原拥有者之身份看，则上至帝王之家、贵族豪门，下及平民百姓。从质地看，大多品质优良，其中更不乏晶莹润泽的羊脂上品。从造型看，不仅有简单明了的片状玉雕，更多隽美秀丽的立体圆雕，而其中多肖生玉雕更是先生藏品中的一大特点。活泼可爱的动物造型，老翁负妻的恬淡戏谑，垂髫小童的憨态可掬，莲台坐佛的宝相庄严，三羊开泰、马上封侯、张仙送子、戏水鸳鸯、俏色蟾蜍、少女晚妆、世间万象、人生百态，尽括其中也。

　　熙墀先生，潜心藏玉凡三十余年，入藏颇丰。所藏古玉，其中多有已面世古玉中之少见、仅见或不见之精品，观书中所示，可谓硕果累累。然先生于三十余年来收藏过程中所历之甘苦，则非亲历而不足以言之。先生收藏古玉始于上世纪六十年代末期，其时由于人所共知的原因，收藏环境极差。于公，国家所设之各级考古发掘单位及各级博物馆的所有业务工作，几乎全都处于瘫痪或停顿状态，更何言及个人收藏。于私，其时不仅收藏环境极差，而且苦于几无发掘出土之玉器作标准可供借鉴。然熙墀先生就是于此中几乎无路、无章之状况下开始了其收藏古玉之行程，这一行就是三十余年。其间的困苦艰辛，则局外人难以知晓；其间的快乐与收获，同样非局外人所能体会。三十余年的收藏历程，如无锲而不舍之心境，持之以恒之毅力，是难以坚持下来的。然熙墀先生不仅坚持了下来，而且乐此不疲。更为难能可贵的是，先生于此独创了一套前所未有的收藏鉴定标准，这一点，极大地丰富了我们的收藏知识。

　　熙墀先生长于鉴赏，精于收藏，爱玉重德。先生数十年潜心此道，精挑细选，严格标准，搜选美玉，集多年心血财力，使数百件玉中精品得以保全。实乃我辈之楷模。

　　今次先生于其私藏之中，择吉公示，使同好得以参考借鉴，世人也可藉此陶冶情操，获得教益。会友共享，优哉乐哉！是以为序。

乙酉年孟冬

于郑州

PREFACE

JIANG Tao

Mr. CHUNG Wah-Pui (Hei-Chi) is deeply fond of jades. He is very experienced and skilled in jade identification and appreciation, and has accumulated a rich collection. Now Mr. Chung selects the most refined from over three hundred collected pieces and prints them, in order to share his treasure with friends in the same line and also with the general public. It is truly fortunate for the world of collectors to have the finest jades from the Hei-Chi collection presented for today's audience and preserved for the future. The publication of this book will surely contribute greatly to the study and appreciation of Chinese jade.

The Hua–Xia civilization is broad and profound with a distant origin and a long development. The ancient sages and our ancestors have left us a wide variety of cultural heritage and relics, which reflect the unique characteristics of the Hua-Xia culture. Of these relics, the jades are more remarkable than other kinds. From ancient times to the present, other sorts of relics have emerged and disappeared, but the jade as an exception has accompanied our life incessantly. The history of the Hua-Xia civilization can be comprehended fully through appreciating jade.

The over two hundred pieces of jade selected by Mr. Chung are significant in many aspects. From the perspective of time frame, they are dated to all the periods, from the prehistoric to the Shang and Zhou, and from the two Hans to the later dynasties of the Tang, Song, Yuan, Ming and Qing. In terms of geographic scope, the distribution of these jades reaches everywhere in the territories of today's China–from the Heilongjiang River, Changbai Mountain and Song–Liao Plains in the north, to the Yangzi River branches and southeast provinces in the south, and from the coastal line in the east, to the Loess Plateau in the west. When looking at the aspect of social rank, the owners of the jades include the royal families, the noble and the rich, and the commoners as well. Speaking of quality, most of these pieces are refined ones and many of them belong to the category of top–quality white jade with translucent luster and warm brilliance. As for morphological types, there are some examples of simple flat shapes, but there are much more elegant and beautiful round figures in this group, of which the outnumbering zoomorphic figures best characterize the Hei-Chi collection. Lastly, the figures selected in this book present splendid scenarios: the lively adorable animals, the playful scene of an old man carrying his wife on his back, the seemingly tangible innocence of young children, the solemnity and reverence of the seated Buddha on a lotus throne, the mandarin ducks playing in water, the toad executed following the natural colors of the stone, the young lady in front of a mirror dressing up at sunset, and also those images as rebuses with auspicious symbolism due to the homophones of their Chinese names, e.g. the three sheep standing for multiple suns, the monkey on horseback for the wish of immediate promotion, and the deity Zhang Xian blessing people to have sons. In short, all manifestations of nature and all phenomena of life have been collected in this book.

Mr. Chung has devoted himself to collecting jades for over 30 years and has been very successful. Of his collected jades, many are rarely seen, or the only remaining piece of the kind, or even never seen before. One can look through this book to recognize his fruitful achievement. However, those who have not had such an experience cannot comprehend all the sorts of sorrows and joys that Mr. Chung has experienced along the journey during the past 30 years. He began collecting jades in the late 1960s when, for reasons that all know, the conditions for relics collection were very frustrating. On the one hand, all the archaeological institutions and museums sponsored by the government were forced to stop their professional work; on the other hand, there were few excavated jades that could be used as reliable references. It was at that time when there was no direction and no guidance, Mr. Chung initiated his exploration of the journey of jade collection, and he has never stopped. None of the difficulties and frustrations, nor the joys and achievements, experienced along this journey can be comprehended by outsiders. Trekking for over 30 years cannot be done without unflagging willpower and persistent perseverance. However, Mr. Chung has journeyed along and enjoyed the process tirelessly. It is even more admirable that Mr. Chung has independently developed an unprecedented set of principles and references for his identification and collection of jades, which has greatly enriched our knowledge of jade collection and should be admired even by professionals like myself.

Mr. Chung is talented in appreciation, expert in collection and cultivating virtues through loving jades. During the past decades, Mr. Chung had tirelessly devoted himself in this field with joy. He is meticulous and unbending in his search of fine jades. After spending years of devotion and extensive personal resources, he has collected and preserved several hundred pieces of refined jades. Mr. Chung should be a role model for all of us.

Now Mr. Chung has selected and published the fines jades from his private collection. This provides an opportunity for people with the same interest to appreciate and learn, and for the general public to cultivate their tastes and characters, and to be educated as well. It is truly a pleasure to have friends to share the joy of this occasion. Let us celebrate it with a glass of wine.

Zhengzhou, Henan
Late winter, 2005

贺《熙墀藏玉》出版

杨伯达

　　2004年7月初，于香港曾与挚友钟华培先生晤见。我们已有两三年间未能谋面，这次相见，钟先生仍像过去一样红光满面，精神焕发，身体健壮，谈笑风生，我也甚感欣慰。我们谈及他所编的《熙墀藏玉》，他用带有厚重粤语腔的普通话解释这是以"字"命名的，我答："听懂了，这很风雅。"他也呵呵地笑了。于是我就翻阅厚厚的两册已选中的玉器照片，从红山文化肖生玉至清代玉雕二百余件赫然在目，令人目不暇接，真是大饱眼福，受益良多。读毕，钟先生即约我为他的《熙墀藏玉》撰写序文。虽然我自揣浅陋，并未专门研究兽类玉雕，但手经目验的出土古代玉雕亦为数不少，多少有些心得，加之又考虑到我们之间经久的真诚友谊，便欣然应诺，为其大作撰一小文以表贺意。

　　我于上世纪80年代初赴港工作时，曾访问过香港收藏家组织 ——"敏求精舍"，结识了不少的收藏家，钟华培先生便是其中的一位。钟华培先生是经营土木建筑工程的企业家，在管理公司事务之暇独钟古玉，热衷收藏。他热情好客，待人和蔼。在我的研究重点转向古玉之后，我们之间往来增多，我们经常交流有关古玉方方面面的观点和经验，他还邀请我到他的住所倾谈至深夜，并取出他珍藏的玉器让我观赏。当时给我印象最深的是一批玉兽，其质地温润而泽，雕工精美细致，拿到手上甚感圆熟光滑，最适把玩摩挲，令人爱不释手，至今记忆犹新。光阴如矢，倏忽已二十载。钟氏收藏日积月累，较过去已益加丰厚。所以我相信他完全具备了遴选精品、编辑成册、付梓印行、公开出版的条件。我也相信，《熙墀藏玉》的问世不仅给读者带来赏玉的乐趣，还可使他们从中获取经验和教益。

　　我看过他那厚厚的两册藏玉彩照之后，深感钟先生在收藏古玉的艰难道路上确实收获不菲，成绩巨大。但是未及详谈他数十年来收藏古玉的苦乐，不过那厚厚的两册彩照及钟先生喜悦的笑容便足以表明他在收藏道路上历经的甘苦，可以说是苦尽甜来，硕果累累。于是我又想到我国考古发掘出土玉器中的缺环，这就是古代兽类玉雕出土的并不多，尤其可供把玩的玉兽清玩几乎不见出土。在缺少出土玉器作标准器的条件下，收藏古玉雕兽类作品要靠独立自主地确立鉴定标准，再去摸索探求，这要付出很大的心血和精力，远远比收集瑞符、祭祀、殓葬等"高古玉器"要困难而又复杂。这不仅需要勇气和信心，更需要锲而不舍、持之以恒的毅力。这条路终于已由钟华培先生走出来了，这是令人由衷敬佩的。

　　最后再次祝贺《熙墀藏玉》的出版发行成功！

2005 年 8 月 30 日

于北京

PRAISE ON THE PUBLICATION OF
JADES FROM THE HEI-CHI COLLECTION

YANG Boda

In early July 2004, I met with my intimate friend Mr. CHUNG Wah–Pui in Hong Kong. Meeting for the first time in two or three years, I was pleased to see his appearance unchanged: he was radiant, energetic, healthy and cheerful. When our talk referred to his book *Jades from the Hei-Chi Collection*, he explained to me in Mandarin with a strong Cantonese accent that the title of this book was after his styled name "Hei-Chi". I replied: "Understood, it's graceful." He laughed loudly. Then I began leafing through the photographs of the jades selected in the two thick volumes. I feasted my eyes upon the over two hundred pieces presented, from zoomorphic figures of the Hongshan culture to the jade sculptures of the Qing dynasty. Though I could not take everything in, the stunning scenes presented taught me greatly. After my reading, Mr. Chung invited me to write a preface for his book. I was aware of my shallowness and also my meager knowledge on the types of zoomorphic figures, but I had indeed gained something from my observation and examination of quite a large amount of unearthed ancient jades, and Mr. Chung and I were true friends of a long period. I therefore gladly accepted the honor to write this short essay to congratulate him on his great work.

When I first went to Hong Kong to work there in the early 1980s, I visited the organization of Hong Kong collectors–"The Min Chiu Society". I became acquainted with many collectors and Mr. Chung was one of them. Mr. Chung is an entrepreneur in the civil engineering field who, in his spare time, pursues his love of ancient jades and eagerly collects them. He is warm-hearted and hospitable, and treats others well. After I turned the focus of my study to ancient jades, our communication increased, frequently exchanging our opinions and experiences on different aspects of ancient jades. He once invited me to his home and we talked till late at night. He also showed me the jades he treasured, and at that time what impressed me the most was a group of animal-shaped figures bearing warm brilliance and exquisite craftsmanship. While holding them in hand, I could feel deeply their masterly carved smoothness. I recall vividly today that these zoomorphic miniatures were so enjoyable to fondle with that I could hardly bear to put them down. Time passes as fast as shooting arrows and it has been twenty years since then. Mr Chung's collection has since accumulated and is becoming richer all the time. I believe this was an ideal time for him to select his most excellent pieces to compile and publish a book. I also believe that the publication of Jades from the Hei-Chi Collection will bring the audience not only the joy of appreciating jades, but also Mr. Chung's experience and knowledge.

After looking through the two thick volumes of color photographs of the jade collection, I feel deeply that Mr. Chung has indeed achieved much on the difficult path of collecting ancient jades. Although this book does not mention in detail the bitterness and happiness of collecting ancient jades he experienced in the past several decades, the two thick volumes of color photographs and Mr. Chung's delighted smile shown in this book are enough to tell us what he has experienced and learned on the path of collecting. We may say now that enjoyment has come after frustration and the achievement is fruitful. I also want to point out a missing link in the archaeologically unearthed jades, namely, that among the unearthed jades, there are a limited number of the types of zoomorphic figures. The zoomorphic miniatures for fondling as enjoyable playthings are especially rare and almost unseen. The condition of lacking unearthed jades as reliable references requires a collector to establish independently some standard of identification first, and then to further explore and search. This process demands a great deal of devotion and energy, and is much more difficult and complicated than collecting the so-called "Remote Ancient Jade" such as auspicious jade, ritual jade or funerary jade. Exploration on this path requires not only courage and belief but also unflagging and incessant perseverance. Mr. Chung has ultimately accomplished the journey, which is truly admirable.

Lastly, let me again congratulate the successful publication of *Jades from the Hei-Chi Collection*.

Beijing
30th August 2005

释香港钟华培先生玉璧刻铭

李学勤

香港锺华培先生所藏的一件玉璧,外径仅3.4厘米,刻铭微小纤细。承姜涛先生以放大照片和拓本见示,得以辨识,试作考释,请读者指教。

铭文在璧肉上环刻,共五字,成半圆形,隶定为:

壬辰,姤易嬃。

"壬"字中间竖笔,由照片看似若向下延伸,其实并不如此,在拓本上便很清楚。

"辰"字上边有一横笔。这样写的"辰",习见于殷墟黄组卜辞[1]。

"姤"字即后妃的"后",这是唐兰先生最先指出的[2]。随后朱凤瀚先生作过详细的论证发挥,他还曾说明类似璧铭这种"姤"字写法,即所从"后"的"口"偏在字左,只见于黄组卜辞[3]。

"易"即"锡"字,众所周知。

最末一字,左从"女",右以"羿"声,是女子私名[4]。"羿"字常见于殷墟卜辞,一般用作地名,是商王田猎场所,近于桵(榆)和良,在早期卜辞里只写作"枈"[5]。"枈"字不识,作为偏旁,其上部有时写成凵、凵、凵、凵、凵等形。"羿"字还可用作动词,如《侯家庄出土之甲骨文字》3有"王其羿舟",而《甲骨文合集》24608有"王其醉舟于滴(漳)",后者"醉"即"寻"加"丙"为声,就读为"寻",训为就(或用)[6]。因此,"羿"也必是"寻"加"枈"为声,"枈"一定是与"寻"同音的古侵部字。这样看来"嬃"字不妨写为"婷",读作"寻"声。

所以璧铭是记在壬辰这一天,王后把这件玉璧赐给名嬃的女子。

整个铭文字体类于黄组卜辞,而且有两字具有黄组的特征,足证璧的时代同于黄组卜辞,也便是商末文丁、帝乙、帝辛之世[7]。

注释:

[1] 李学勤、彭裕商《殷墟甲骨分期研究》,第174页,上海古籍出版社,1996年。

[2]《安阳殷墟五号墓座谈纪要》,《考古》1977年第3期。

[3] 朱凤瀚《论卜辞与商金文中的"后"》,《古文字研究》第19辑,中华书局,1992年。

[4] 关于殷商女名,参看李学勤《考古发现与古代姓氏制度》,《考古》1987年第3期。

[5] 李学勤《殷代地理简论》,第17~18页,科学出版社,1959年。

[6] 李学勤《续释"寻"字》,《故宫博物院院刊》2000年第6期。

[7] 黄组包括三世,参看常玉芝《商代周祭制度》,第291~301页,中国社会科学出版社,1987年。

DECIPHERING THE INSCRIPTIONS ON THE *BI*-DISK OF MR. CHUNG WAH-PUI IN HONG KONG

LI Xuəqin

The bi-disk collected by Mr. CHUNG Wah–Pui in Hong Kong is small in size, with an outer diameter of only 3.4 cm, and bears tiny and thin inscription. After Mr. JIANG Tao showed me an enlarged photograph and rubbing of the inscriptions, I could identify it. I am now trying to decipher the inscription and await critiques.

The inscription are incised on the middle part of the disk's body and arranged in a semi-circular shape. There are five characters in total and they are deciphered as follows:

ren chen, hou yi xun (壬辰，姤易嬃).

The character "*ren*" has a vertical stroke in the middle of the character, which seems to extend downward and across the bottom horizontal stroke from the photograph. But the rubbing clearly shows that the vertical stroke is actually not extended.

The character "*chen*" has a horizontal stroke at the top of the character. This style of writing is often seen in oracle bone inscriptions of Group Huang at Yin Ruins [1].

The character "*hou*" is the character "*hou*" (后) for queen, an interpretation being first proposed by Prof. TANG Lan [2]. Since then, Prof. ZHU Fenghan has elaborated on this point with more detail. The character "*hou*" on the disk is structured in a distinctive style, namely that the square shaped radical 姤 with the part 后 is placed on the left side of the character. According to Prof. Zhu, similar styles of structuring this character are only seen on inscriptions of Group Huang [3].

The character "*yi*" is the character "*ci*" (锡), and its meaning, "to bestow", is well known.

The last character "*xun*" is a private name of a woman [4], with its right-side radical bearing the significance " 女 " ("female") and its left-side radical "将" giving the pronunciation "*xun*" of the character. The character "将" is often seen in oracle bone inscriptions at Yin Ruins and usually used as a place name, referring to the hunting fields for Shang kings. This character, similar to characters "*yu*" 桵(榆) and "*liang*" (良), was only written as "米" in early oracle bone inscriptions [5]. The character "米" is yet to be deciphered, but, as a radical, it is sometimes written in the shapes of ⼝, ⼝, ⼝, ⼝ and ⼝. The character "将" can also be used as a verb. For example, there is a phrase "king 将 boat" in Houjiazhuang chutu zhi jiaguwen (Oracle Bone Inscriptions from Houjiazhuang) 3. In Jiaguwen heji (Compilation of Oracle Bone Inscriptions), 24608, there is also a phrase "king 辝 boat at 滴 (Zhang River)". In the latter phrase, the character is composed of the radical " 寻 " and "㐬" as its pronunciation radical, and should be pronounced "*xun*", with the meaning "to approach" or "to arrive" [6]. Therefore, the character "将" should also be composed of " 寻 " and "米" as its pronunciation radical, and "米" must be an ancient homophone of the character " 寻 ". Therefore, the last character on the disk might be written in the shape "婨" and pronounced "*xun*".

In summary, the inscriptions on the disk record an event that on the day "*ren chen*", a queen bestowed this disk to a woman named 嬃.

The writing style of the inscriptions on the disk is similar to that of oracle bone inscriptions of Group Huang; in fact, two characters out of five bear the exact characteristics of Group Huang inscriptions. The evidence is sufficient to confirm that the date of the disk in question is the same as that of Group Huang inscriptions, namely, the period of the last three Shang kings: Wen-Ding, Di-Yi and Di-Xin [7].

References and Notes:

1. LI Xueqin and PENG Yushang, *Yinxu jiaguwen fenqi yanjiu*, p. 174, Shanghai Guji Press, 1996.

2. "Anyang Yinxu wuhao mu zuotan jiyao", Kaogu, 1977/3.

3. ZHU Fenghan, "Lun puci yu Shang jinwen zhongde 'hou'", *Guwenzi Yanjiu*, Vol. 19, Zhonghua Press, 1992.

4. As for women's name in the Shang period, please see LI Xueqin, "Kaogu faxian yu gudai xingshi zhidu", *Kaogu*, 1987/3.

5. LI Xueqin, *Yindai dili jianlun*, pp. 17-18, Kexue Press, 1959.

6. LI Xueqin, "Xushi 'xun' zi", *Gugong Bowuyuan Yuankan*, 2000/6.

7. Inscriptions of Group Huang include three reign titles, please see CHANG Yuzhi, *Shangdai zhouji zhidu*, pp. 291-301, Zhongguo Shehui Kexue Press, 1987.

汉代圆雕玉器的艺术风采

刘云辉

  汉代是中国玉雕艺术的发达时期。其显著标志,一是汉代玉器制作规模宏大;二是新疆和阗美玉,随着丝绸之路的开通,能够更为顺畅地输入中原,因此,汉代和阗玉所占比重增大;三是汉代在继承战国的基础上,玉雕工艺又有了新的发展,高浮雕和圆雕器增多,而圆雕玉器的艺术成就颇高,在中国玉雕史上占有特别重要的地位。

  迄今为止,有明确出土记录的汉代圆雕玉器主要有:1966年在陕西省咸阳原新庄村汉元帝渭陵建筑基址内发现的玉羽人骑翼马[1]。1972年在上述同一地点内出土的玉鹰、玉熊、玉戴冠俑头和两件玉辟邪[2]。1972年在陕西省蒲城县贾曲村西汉建筑基址内出土一件大型玉牛[3]。1983年在陕西省西安市南郊沙坡西汉墓中出土一对形体较大的玉猪[4]。1981年在西安市西郊三桥西汉晚期墓出土一件獬豸[5]。1978年在陕西省宝鸡市北郊金河砖厂的西汉晚期墓中出土一件大型玉辟邪[6]。1968年在河北省满城一号汉墓出土的一件凭几而坐的玉人[7]。1977年山东省巨野县红土山汉墓出土的小型玉马[8]。1983年广州南越王墓出土的玉舞人[9]。1982年江苏省徐州市北洞山汉墓出土一件大型玉熊[10]。1994年江苏徐州狮子山楚王陵出土一件大型玉豹[11]。1984年江苏省扬州市甘泉老虎墩东汉墓出土一件辟邪形玉壶[12]。上述圆雕玉器虽然在目前所出土的数量众多的汉代玉器中所占比例很小,但多数圆雕作品均是采用新疆和阗美玉雕琢。尤其是汉元帝渭陵和老虎墩东汉墓出土的圆雕作品,玉质上乘、晶莹鲜润,玉雕气派宏大,内涵丰富,而且造型生动,纹饰流畅,抛磨光洁,是汉代玉器中的杰作。这些圆雕真正突破了先秦玉雕图案化风格的樊篱,展现了汉代玉器高度发达的工艺水平。

  因工作关系,作者曾多次有机会对渭陵陵园出土的6件圆雕玉器作全方位的观察,并拍摄了这些玉器所有细部的照片,也常常被这些作品的艺术感染力所吸引。

  近年来,作者曾多次赴港,鉴赏了熙墀先生所收藏的玉器,特别是对若干件汉代圆雕作品,进行了仔细反复观察,留下了深刻印象。如跪姿玉羽人晶莹的玉质,生动的造型,流畅的纹饰,以及细腻的处理手法。玉羽人骑辟邪中的羽人神情之诡秘,辟邪形象之凶猛,胸肌之发达,这一切至今仍然难以忘怀。圆雕玉象的高大宽厚,神情安详,憨态可掬。体态肥美的圆雕玉奔羊等,均是形神兼备,栩栩如生的佳作。还有一件作行走状的圆雕绿松石辟邪,更令人赞叹不已。总而言之,熙墀先生所收藏的汉代圆雕玉器,一是数量多、种类杂,大象、奔羊、玉虎,增补了西汉出土圆雕玉器的空白。跪姿圆雕玉羽人和行走状绿松石辟邪也是首次发现的。二是造型之生动,若能亲眼观赏,必为其高超的艺术美丽所感染。三是工艺精湛,从轮廓处理、装饰纹样雕琢、表面抛光等方面观察,均十分考究。笔者认为研究汉代玉雕,熙墀先生所收藏的圆雕玉器是相当重要不可或缺的实物资料。它们与有明确出土记录的圆雕玉器一同构成了汉代圆雕玉器迷人的艺术风采。

注释：

[1] 王丕忠《咸阳新庄出土的玉奔马》，《文物》，1979年第3期，第86页。

[2] 张子波《咸阳新庄出土的四件汉代圆雕玉器》，《文物》，1979年第2期第60页。又见咸阳市博物馆《汉元帝渭陵调查记》，《考古与文物》1980年第1期，第38～41页。

[3] 陶仲云《蒲城县出土的汉代玉雕水牛》，《考古与文物》，1981年第2期，第110页。

[4] 西安市文管会《玉器》图版82，陕西旅游出版社，1992年。

[5] 西安市文管会《玉器》图版87，陕西旅游出版社，1992年。

[6] 王宏武《宝鸡金河砖厂汉墓》，《文物资料丛刊》4，236～237页，1981年。

[7] 卢兆荫《中国玉器全集》4，秦汉南北朝，图版九二，河北美术出版社，1993年。

[8] 卢兆荫《中国玉器全集》4，秦汉南北朝，图版一一六，河北美术出版社，1993年。

[9] 广州西汉南越王墓博物馆、香港中文大学文物馆·求知雅集·两木出版社《南越王墓玉器》，图版234～235，1994年。

[10] 徐州博物馆、南京大学历史系考古专业《徐州北洞山西汉楚王墓》，124页，图一〇二：5、彩版五九：3，文物出版社，2003年。

[11] 中国国家博物馆、中国文物交流中心等《世纪国宝Ⅱ》，图版56，生活·读书·新知三联书店，2005年。

[12] 扬州博物馆、天长市博物馆编《汉广陵国玉器》，图版122，文物出版社，2003年。

THE ARTISTIC ELEGANCE OF THE JADE ROUND FIGURES FROM THE HAN PERIOD

LIU Yunhui

The art of jade carving in China flourished during the Han dynasties, and this period featured a series of distinctive characters. Firstly, the scale of jade making was expanded broadly during the Han period. Secondly, with the opening of the Silk Road, the fine jade material from Khotan in Xinjiang could be transported much more easily to the Central Plains, which resulted in the increase in the proportion of Khotan jade among the jade material. Thirdly, the craftsmanship of jade carving was further developed on the technical basis of the Warring States, and this development was characterized by the increase of carvings in high relief and carvings in the round. The artistic achievement of round figure carvings during the Han period is fairly high and occupies a very important position in the history of jade making in China.

As of today, the round jade figures that are clearly recorded from archaeological excavations mainly include the following items:

(1) The winged figure riding on a winged horse, discovered in 1966 from the base platform of the architecture on the Weiling-mausoleum for Emperor Yuan of the Western Han located at the Xinzhuangcun in Xianyang, Shaanxi Province [1].

(2) A group of jade figures including eagle, bear, the head of a tomb-figure with crown, and two pieces of *bixie*-chimera figure unearthed in 1972 from the same location introduced above [2].

(3) The large bull figure unearthed in 1972 from the architectural platform dated to the Western Han and located at Jiaqucun in Pucheng, Shaanxi Province [3].

(4) A pair of large pig figures unearthed in 1983 from the tomb of the Western Han at Shapo in the western suburb of Xi'an City, Shaanxi Province [4].

(5) The *xiezhi*-guarding animal figure unearthed in 1981 from the tomb of the late Western Han at Sanqiao in the western suburb of Xi'an City, Shaanxi Province [5].

(6) The large *bixie*-chimera figure unearthed in 1978 from the tomb of the late Western Han located in the Brick Factory at Jinhe in the northern suburb of Xianyang City, Shaanxi Province [6].

(7) The human figure sitting at a *ji*-small table unearthed in 1968 from the Han Tomb No. 1 at Mancheng, Hebei Province [7].

(8) The small horse figurine unearthed in 1977 from the Han tomb at Hongtushan in Juye, Shandong Province [8].

(9) The dancing figure unearthed in 1983 from the Nanyue King's Tomb of the Western Han located in Guangzhou, Guangdong Province [9].

(10) The large bear figure unearthed in 1982 from the Han tomb at Beidongshan in Xuzhou, Jiangsu Province [10].

(11) The large leopard figure unearthed in 1994 from the Han Mausoleum of King Chu at Shizishan in Xuzhou, Jiangsu Province [11].

(12) The *bixie*-shaped ewer unearthed in 1984 from the Eastern Han tomb at Laohudun of Ganquan in Yangzhou, Jiangsu Province [12].

The above-mentioned jade figures only contribute limitedly to the huge amount of excavated Han jades, but most of them are shaped from the fine Khotan material of Xinjiang. The first and last items listed above, the winged figure on a winged horse and the ewer, deserve special attention. The two pieces, both shaped from top-quality material with brilliant luster, were not only designed with a grand and sophisticated style, but also vividly formed, smoothly decorated and finely polished, therefore can be treated as the models for Han jades. These round figures have broken through the constraints of the patterned style on the pre-Qin jades, and represent the highly developed craftsmanship of the Han period.

Thanks to the responsibilities of my occupation, I have had many opportunities to observe closely the six round figures unearthed from the Weiling Mausoleum Park and take pictures of all the details. I was often attracted to these jades by their artistic elegance.

In recent years, I have visited Hong Kong many times. During my visits, I studied the Hei-Chi collection and, particularly, examined the Han round figures over and over carefully. The deep impression left by these figures is unforgettable. For example, the kneeling plumed female figure attracted me with its brilliant stone quality, lively shaping, smooth decoration and delicate methods of treatment. Another example was the plumed rider on *bixie*-chimera, which stood out of the group by the secretive expression of the plumed rider, the ferocious look of the *bixie* and the depiction of the well-developed muscles on the animal's chest. Other examples include the grand but adorable elephant as well as the fat but graceful running ram, which have been given life by being created with both morphological accuracy and inner spirit. I was even further struck with awe by the turquoise *bixie*-chimera figure in a walking posture. In summary, the round figures of the Han period in the Hei-Chi collection are significant in several aspects. Firstly, the number of round figures is large and their types are varied. The images of elephant, running ram, and tiger fulfill a blank in the excavated round figures dated to the Western Han. The kneeled *plumed* figure and turquoise *bixie* are also the first of their types known to the world. Secondly, the liveliness of the modeling of the round figures gives everyone who views them a deep impression of their outstanding artistic beauty. Lastly, the craftsmanship is skillful. The carvings are exquisite in all aspects, from the shaping of the outline, to the incising and chiseling of the decoration, and to the polishing of the surface. I believe that the round figures collected by Mr. Chung are important and indispensable material for the study of jade figures of the Han period. Together with the round figures from clearly recorded excavations, they have revealed to us the fascinating artistic elegance of round figures from the Han period.

References Cited
1. WANG Peizhong, "Xianyang Xinzhuang chutu de yu benma", *Wenwu*, 1979/3: 86.
2. ZHANG Zipo, "Xianyang Xinzhuang chutu de sijian handai yuandiao yuqi", *Wenwu*, 1979/2: 60; also Xianyang Bowuguan, "Han Yuandi Weiling diaochaji", Kaogu yu *Wenwu*, 1980/1: 38-41.
3. TAO Zhongyun, "Puchengxian chutu de handai yudiao shuiniu", *Kaogu yu Wenwu*, 1981/2: 110.
4. Xi'anshi Wenguanhui, *Yuqi*, Plate 82, Shaanxi Luyou Press, 1992.

5. Xi'anshi Wenguanhui, *Yuqi*, Plate 87, Shaanxi Luyou Press, 1992.

6. WANG Hongwu, "Baoji Jinhe zhuanchang hanmu", *Wenwu ziliao congkan*, Vol. 4, 1981, pp. 236-237.

7. LU Zhaoyin, *Zhongguo yuqi quanji*, Vol. 4, Plate 92, Hebei meishu Press, 1993.

8. LU Zhaoyin, *Zhongguo yuqi quanji*, Vol. 4, Plate 116, Hebei meishu Press, 1993.

9. Guangxi Nanyuewang Bowuguan, Xianggang Zhongwen Daxue Wenwuguan, *Nanyue Wang Mu Yuqi*, Qiuzhiyaji-Liangmu Press, Plate 234-235, 1994.

10. Xuzhou Bowuguan, Nanjingdaxue Lishixi Kaogu Zhuanye, *Xuzhou Beidongshan Xihan Chuwangmu*, p. 124, Figure 103, Color Plate 59:3, Wenwu Press, 2003.

11. Zhongguo Guojia Bowuguan, Zhongguo Wenwu Jiaoliu Zhongxin, *Shiji Guobao*, Vol. II, Plate 56, Sanlian Press, 2005.

12. Yangzhou Bowuguan, Tianchangshi Bowuguan, *Han Guanglingguo Yuqi*, Plate 122, Wenwu Press, 2003.

熙墀藏玉之研究

姜 涛

　　熙墀先生是一位国内外知名的资深收藏家，且和蔼可亲，平易近人。我与先生相识于上世纪九十年代初。曾有机会多次鉴赏过先生历经三十余年所收藏的许多玉器珍品，不仅大饱了眼福，而且给我留下了极深的印象，使我受益良多。去年年初，先生嘱我与陕西刘云辉一起，协助对其所藏之玉器进行系统整理，并着手编著《熙墀藏玉》一书。初时，我多有诚惶诚恐、惴惴不安之感。我虽因工作关系，多年来对玉器研究领域稍有涉猎，但如要我担纲主持对这样一批年代、地域涵盖广，门类、工艺复杂，质优、量大的玉器藏品进行系统整理并编著出版，自觉有学识浅陋、力有不逮之感。然作为忘年之交，一者不忍拂先生殷殷之意，二者对自己而言，也是一次增长学识的机会，故而应允了下来。历经年余，终成完稿。付梓之余，自觉对此批玉器稍有心得，故借此书出版之际言之。

　　熙墀藏玉，最大之特点是涵盖极广。广的含义包括了地域、年代、族属、等级、功能、用途、风格、工艺等诸方面。从地域言，几乎涵盖了我国版图的全部所在。从年代言，由距今5000余年的东北红山、南方江淮始，经商、西周、东周、两汉、魏晋、唐宋、元、明至清朝止，均有涉及。如本书所收史前玉器中的四件红山玉——三联璧、猪龙、双系璧及镯形器，质佳形美，于发掘品中也是极少见的，称之为红山珍品，毫不为过。还有一件应属史前江淮凌家滩文化的虎首形璜，其颇具灵性的双虎首及以阴线示出的肥大前肢特征明显，对正式发掘品而言，又多了一个印证。还有一件属黄河流域龙山文化中晚期的青玉双孔钺，也是不可多得之物。另有一件值得注意的史前玉器是属石家河文化的虎首饰，其与发掘出土的几件同类器有所不同。发掘品从侧面观察多为长方圆角形，而此件形制偏扁圆。其纹饰及工艺的处理虽与上海博物馆藏虎头饰多有相似，但细部处理还是稍有不同。无论如何，此件虎首饰对石家河文化玉器的研究提供了新的角度，如有机会将此器做一次工艺痕迹方面的检测，则更能说明问题。

　　熙墀先生所藏三代玉器中更是精品多多。如用优质和阗白玉精琢而成的龙形璜，质润工佳，是商玉中的上乘之作。其原器主极可能是出自商王室一族。另一件刻铭玉璧所记，经著名学者李学勤先生考证，确认为是商末文丁、帝乙、帝辛三世六十七年间之物，其铭记载了某王后赐此璧于一名嬉的女子。商代刻铭玉器存世者本就无多，能确认是商末之时者，更是绝无仅有。此璧的学术价值之高，不言而喻。商器中值得一提的还有四件松石精品，人、龙、熊、鹦鹉，形态各异。集四件松石精品藏于一人亦十分难得。西周时期的人龙合雕佩、双面施纹的圆形龙纹佩、凤鸟纹箍形器等，相信均是西周时公侯级高级贵族用物。而圆雕犀牛、半圆雕牛首形佩则更是少见。

　　春秋战国一段中精品多楚器及楚式器。属春秋时期的虎形佩、兽面形饰、管形龙纹等一批精品均等同或优于淅川下寺楚墓、宝相寺黄君孟夫妇墓、太原金胜村墓等所出同类器。尤为值得关注的是数件镶嵌于它物之上的玉件，如用高浮雕手法满工而制的弧面回首虎形饰、白玉龙纹拱形饰、兽面纹拱形饰，于发掘品及馆藏精品中也是少之又少的。战国段中属片雕类的，有刻有编号的一环一璧、有青白玉质的屈体龙形佩、镂空人龙合纹璧；属楚玉的白玉龙凤螭合雕佩及双面施游丝线纹的凤形佩；属松石类的镂空双身龙形佩、团身螭虎佩；圆雕类中属绚索纹龙形佩最佳，此件在面世的同类龙佩中，实属上上之选。

汉玉中的多件圆雕，绝不亚于目前已知的发掘及馆藏汉玉。正如刘云辉所言"研究汉代玉雕，熙墀先生所收藏的圆雕玉器是相当重要不可或缺的实物资料，他们与有明确出土纪录的圆雕玉器一同构成了汉代圆雕玉器迷人的艺术风采"。

言及熙墀藏玉的族属，有史前分处于四方的各部族之物。三代时，有夏、商、周、楚、吴等族中上层人物所用的佳品。更有汉以后的汉、满、蒙、契丹、女真等族人的遗存。

言及用途方面，熙墀藏玉中既有登大雅之堂而用的礼玉，又多日常生活所用的装饰类玉；既有可供把玩、观赏的案头摆设，又有供于佛堂之上的莲台坐佛；有文人书生必用的笔搁、纸镇，求官所喜的马上封侯，又有寻常百姓喜爱的麻姑献寿、连生贵子。宫廷御用之精品，普通妇女的头面饰物等，集于一堂，洋洋大观。正如我在序中所言"世间万象，人生百态，尽括其中也"。

熙墀藏玉的另一大特点，就是多立体圆雕，多肖生玉雕。尤其是南北朝至唐、宋、元、明、清时期的藏品，几乎全是此类。而这一段，尤其是宋、元、明、清时期，少有正式发掘出土品可供验证、参照。故言之，熙墀藏玉不仅在研究汉代玉雕时不可或缺，而且在研究唐、宋、元、明、清玉雕时，更是弥足珍贵。

借用杨伯达先生贺词中的一句话，"《熙墀藏玉》的问世不仅给读者带来赏玉的乐趣，还可使他们从中获取经验和教益"。

A STUDY ON JADES FROM THE HEI-CHI COLLECTION

JIANG Tao

Mr. CHUNG Wah–Pui is a senior collector well-known in China and overseas. He is affable and easy to approach. I became acquainted with him in the early 1990s. Since then, I have had the chance to appreciate many precious jades from his collection of over 30 years. That experience has not only been a delight for my eyes but has also deeply impressed me and taught me a lot. Early last year, Mr. Chung requested the assistance of Mr. LIU Yunhui and myself with conducting systematic research on his jade collection, and compiling the book Jades from the Hei-Chi Collection. At first, I was struck with reverence and awe, and extremely afraid. Due to my work, I have had some experience in the study of jade in the past years. However I felt unprepared and incapable when I was asked to take charge of the systematic research and publication of such a large group of jades, which cover a wide range of time periods and regions, consist of complicated types and craftsmanship, and are of excellent quality and large quantity. However, I could not reject Mr. Chung's request for two reasons. Not only am I a good friend of Mr. Chung's of a much younger age but this would also be an opportunity for me to enrich my knowledge on the subject. After working for over a year, I have now accomplished the task. Prior to the publication of this book, I would like to tell the audience what I have learned from the study of this group of jades.

The most distinctive characteristic of the Hei-Chi collection is its broad coverage. Its broadness refers to many aspects, including geographic distribution, chronological length, attributes of ethnicity, social hierarchy, function, usage, style and craftsmanship. Speaking of distribution, the original locations of the jades cover almost all the geographic regions of China. As for the chronological length, the dates of the jades cross all the major prehistoric and historical periods, from the Hongshan culture in northeastern China and the Jiang-Huai region in the south dating to over 5000 years ago, through the dynasties of the Shang, Western Zhou, Eastern Zhou, Western Han, Eastern Han, Wei-and-Jin, Tang-and-Song, Yuan, Ming, and to the Qing dynasty. For example, the four jade pieces from the Hongshan culture, namely, the three-ring pendant, the coiled pig-dragon *jue*-slit disk, the *bi*-disk with two suspension holes and the bracelet, are excellent in quality and beautiful in presentation, and are rarely seen even among excavated jades. Therefore, it is not extravagant to treat them as the finest pieces of the Hongshan. There is also a tiger-head huang-segment supposedly from the prehistoric Lingjiatan culture in the Jiang-Huai region, which verifies one more time the formally excavated material with its lively carved double tiger-head and incised big forelimbs. Without exaggerating, it can be said that this piece is one of the finest tiger-shaped figures from prehistory. There is also a green jade yue-axe with double holes, which belongs to the Longshan culture of the Yellow River branches and is also an exceptional piece. Another remarkable prehistoric piece is the tiger-shaped ornament from the Shijiahe culture. This tiger ornament distinguishes itself from several other excavated tiger ornaments by its shape. The cross-section of the excavated pieces is rectangular in shape with rounded corners, but this Shijiahe piece has a nearly oval shape. The tiger ornament from the Shijiahe is similar to the piece kept in Shanghai Museum in terms of their decoration and treatment, but the details are slightly different. Nonetheless, this tiger ornament provides the study of the Shijiahe jades with a new perspective, and it will be even more informative if a test on its processing traces can be conducted.

There are more excellent examples among the jades dated to the Three-dynasties in the Hei-Chi collection. For instance, the dragon-shaped *huang*-segment is one of the best Shang jades, considering its top-quality Khotan material and fine craftsmanship. The original owner of this segment was probably a member of the royal family of the Shang. More important than this segment are the inscriptions identified on a *bi*-disk and, according to the renowned scholar

Prof. LI Xueqin, can be firmly dated to a short period of 67 years during the reigns of the last three kings of the Shang: Wen-Ding, Di-Yi and Di-Xin. The inscriptions record the event of a queen bestowing the disk to a woman with a name pronounced "xun". The known extant jades from the Shang with inscriptions are rare, and those which can be firmly dated to the ending period of the Shang are definitely exceptional. Therefore, the great academic significance of this disk is self-evident. There are also four fine pieces of turquoise carvings among the Shang jades with the shapes of human, dragon, bear and parrot, respectively. It is very difficult for one person to collect four fine pieces of turquoise figurines. Of the jades dating to the Western Zhou, several pieces should have originally belonged to some high aristocrats with the rank of duke or marquis, including the pendant with combined human and dragon design, the round pendant with incised dragon on both sides, and the tube-shaped fitting with a phoenix design. There are also some rarely seen pieces among the Western Zhou jades, including the rhinoceros figure in the round and the semi-circular pendant with bull-head wrought in the round.

The jades dating to the Spring-and-Autumn period in the Hei-Chi collection are characterized by the phenomenon that the finest pieces and jades with Chu style are outnumbered. In Chinese archaeology, some top-quality jades datable to this period have been unearthed from several famous burials, including the tombs of Chu at Xiasi in Xichuan, Henan Province, the tomb for Viscount Meng and his wife of Huang at Baoxiangsi in Guangshan, Henan Province, and the tombs of Jin at Jinshengcun in Taiyuan, Shanxi Province. A group of the finest pieces from the Hei-Chi collection, however, are as good as or even better than those excavated pieces of the same kind. These pieces include the tiger-shaped pendant, the animal-mask shaped ornament, and the tube-shaped *jue*-slit disk with dragon design. Some small pieces made as fittings or inlays for larger items deserve special attention, and they are definitely the least known examples in the archaeological assemblages and museum collections. These fittings include the tiger ornament with arched body, back-turned head and fully covered decoration in high relief, the arch-shaped white jade ornament with dragon design, and the arch-shaped ornament with animal-mask design. The finest pieces dating to the Warring States period can be introduced according to their types. Of the type of the flat carvings, there are two pieces, a *huan*-ring and a *bi*-disk, that are both marked with number characters. Also of this type are a pale green jade pendant with a curved dragon shape, and a bi-disk with combined openwork human and dragon figures. Of the type of jades with Chu style, there is a white jade pendant with combined images of dragon, phoenix and feline, and also a phoenix-shaped pendant with hair-thin curved lines incised on both sides. Of the type of turquoise pieces, there is an openwork pendant in the shape of a dragon with two bodies, and also a feline pendant with tucked body. Among the round figures, the best one is the dragon-shaped pendant with its coiled body like a twisted rope. This piece is undeniably one of the best among the existing dragon pendants of the same kind and same period.

The round figures dating to the Han dynasties in the Hei-Chi collection are in no way inferior to the known Han jades from excavations or in museum collections. As Mr. Liu Yunhui has said it in his following essay, "(T)he round figures collected by Mr. Chung are important and indispensable material for the study of jade figures of the Han period. Together with the round figures from clearly recorded excavations, they have revealed to us the fascinating artistic elegance of round figures from the Han period."

From the perspective of the ethnic attributes, the Hei-Chi collection has taken in specimens belonging to different ethnic groups living in different places. Among those dating to the "Three-dynasties", there are fine pieces owned by the high-ranking people from the clans of the Xia, Shang, Zhou, Chu and Wu. There are also remains dated to the post-Han periods that belonged to the peoples of the Han, the Manchurians, the Mongols, the Khitan and the Nuchen.

Speaking of function, the Hei-Chi collection comprises jades made for many different purposes and circumstances. There are not only ritual jades for grand and elegant ceremonies, but also decorative ornaments for everyday life. One can find from the collection pieces ranging from playthings for fondling and appreciation in the study room, to a seated Buddha on a lotus throne for worship in the temple. The scholars might like the brush holders. Those who pursue official posts would love the figure of a monkey on horseback ("ma shang feng hou", homophonic to the four characters meaning "immediately being conferred nobility"). There are also other sorts of carvings as auspicious symbols for ordinary people, e.g. the figure of immortal lady Magu celebrating longevity, and the figure of a little boy sitting on a lotus ("lian sheng gui zi" for "having precious sons one after another"). Further, there are refined pieces for the royal court and decorative ornaments for ordinary women. In short, when collected together, these pieces present a truly splendid scenario. As I said in the preface I wrote for this book, "all manifestations of nature and all phenomena of life have been collected in this book."

Another significant characteristic of the Hei-Chi collection is its remarkable amount of round figures and animal-shaped sculptures. This is especially true of the pieces dated to the periods from the Southern-and-Northern dynasties to the dynasties of the Tang, Song, Yuan, Ming and Qing, which are almost all figures of these types. In historical archaeology, particularly for the periods from the Song to the Qing, the number of scientifically excavated jades is too limited to provide reliable references. It is from this point of view that the Hei-Chi collection is truly precious and indispensable for the study of jade sculptures dating to the Han dynasties, and it is more so for the study of jade sculptures dating to the dynasties of the Tang, Song, Yuan, Ming and Qing.

To conclude, I would like to borrow a line from Prof. YANG Boda's praising essay: "(T)he publication of Jades from the Hei-Chi Collection will bring the audience not only the joy of appreciating jades, but also Mr. Chung's experience and knowledge."

彩 色 图 版
Color Photograghs

三联璧
THREE-RING PENDANT

新石器时代 红山文化(公元前 4000～前 3000 年)
青白玉 半透明
高 8.8、最宽处 4.2、厚 0.5 厘米

Neolithic, Hongshan culture (c.4000 - 3000 BC)
Translucent pale green jade
Height, 8.8 cm; width, 4.2 cm; thickness, 0.5 cm

三璧垂直相连，由上至下，大小依次递增。三璧
之间以凹口相隔。三璧两侧外缘均呈弧线状。上
璧上缘正中为系绳处。此器形制与辽宁阜新胡头
沟 3 号墓所出三联璧相近，当为存世品中少见的
红山玉器珍品。

参见：

1.辽宁省文物考古研究所《牛河梁红山文化遗址与玉器精粹》，
图版 17、第 58 页。文物出版社，1997 年。

2.中国玉器全集编辑委员会《中国玉器全集》(1) 原始社会，图
版 7、第 7 页，文、第 219 页。河北美术出版社，1992 年。

双系璧
BI-DISK WITH TWO SUSPENSION HOLES

新石器时代 红山文化（公元前4000～前3000年）
青白玉 半透明
外径10.5、内径4.6、厚0.5厘米

Neolithic, Hongshan culture (c. 4000 - 3000 BC)
Translucent pale green jade
Diameter, 10.5 cm; perforation diameter, 4.6 cm;
thickness, 0.5 cm

外廓方圆，边缘稍薄，上端有横列双钻孔，器表
抛磨光素，局部有沁。此器与辽宁建平牛河梁第
5地点1号冢M1（牛521M1）墓主头部两侧的玉璧
形制相近，当为存世的红山玉器珍品。

参见：
辽宁省文物考古研究所《牛河梁红山文化遗址与玉器精粹》，图
版8、第54页。文物出版社，1997年。

镯形器
BRACELET

新石器时代 红山文化（公元前4000～前3000年）
青白玉 半透明
外径7.0、内径6.0、厚0.4厘米

Neolithic, Hongshan culture (c. 4000 - 3000 BC)
Translucent pale green jade
Diameter, 7.0 cm; perforation diameter, 6.0 cm;
thickness, 0.4 cm

器表抛磨光洁，横截面为钝三角形，制作精细。此
件器物造型及制作工艺与牛河梁第3地点9号墓所
出玉镯极为相近，当为存世红山玉器中的精品。

参见：
1.《玲珑玉雕》，图版137，第160页。香港大学美术博物馆，1996
年。
2.辽宁省文物考古研究所《牛河梁红山文化遗址玉器精粹》，图
版23、第61页。文物出版社，1997年。

兽形玦
ZOOMORPHIC JUE-SLIT DISK (COILED PIG-DRAGON)

新石器时代 红山文化（公元前4000～前3000年）
青玉 局部有沁
高10.0、宽7.2、厚2.5～3.8厘米

Neolithic, Hongshan culture (c. 4000 - 3000 BC)
Pale green jade with partial discoloration
Height, 10.0 cm; width, 7.2 cm; thickness, 2.5 - 3.8 cm

兽首肥大，双耳耸立，圆目，吻部前突，鼻间多
皱纹。首尾相连处缺而不断。整器呈"C"形蜷曲，
躯体肥厚。背部近颈处一圆穿，器中一大圆穿，均
对钻而成。从器表观察，似传世已久。依其形制，
此器属红山文化兽形玦，亦称"猪龙"。此器与辽
宁省博物馆藏玉兽形玦极似，当为传世藏品中不
多见的珍品。

参见：
中国玉器全集编辑委员会《中国玉器全集》(1)原始社会，图
版24、第20页，文、第224页。河北美术出版社，1992年。

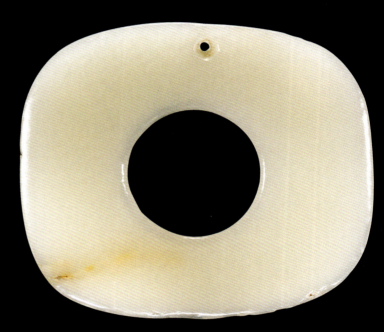

玦形佩
JUE-SLIT DISK

新石器时代 东北地区（公元前3500～前1600年）
青玉
外径3.3、厚0.6厘米

North-eastern China (c. 3500 - 1600 BC)
Green jade Neolithic
Diameter, 3.3 cm; thickness, 0.6 cm

全器经过抛磨。器表一面凸起，一面平直，口处切
割不甚规整。依材质及形制分析，其当为东北地
区新石器时代晚期之物。

白玉系璧
SUSPENSION *BI*-DISK

新石器时代 东北地区（公元前3500～前1600年）
白玉 半透明
高6.5、宽7.5、厚0.4厘米

Neolithic, Northeastern China (c. 3500 - 1600 BC)
Translucent white jade
Height, 6.5 cm; width, 7.5 cm; thickness, 0.4 cm

整器作长方圆角状，上端正中有一单面钻系孔。
质地白中泛青。依形制，此器当为东北地区新石
器时代稍晚时期的遗物。

双联璧
DOUBLE *BI*-DISK

新石器时代 东北地区 (公元前3500～前1600年)
青玉
高 8.3、宽 4.8、厚 0.3 厘米

Neolithic North-eastern China (c. 3500 - 1600 BC)
Green jade
Height, 8.3 cm; width, 4.8 cm; thickness, 0.3 cm

上小下大，上端正中有单面钻系孔。双璧间以凹口相隔。此种形制的双联璧及多联璧最早应见于东北嫩江流域的新开流文化，其后在红山文化、大汶口文化中晚期以及夏家店文化时期均有出现。此器当为东北地区新石器时代晚期的遗物。

齿牙璧
NOTCHED *BI*-DISK

新石器时代 江淮地区（公元前3500~前2200年）
青玉
外径16.6、内径7.6、厚0.4~0.8厘米

Green jade
Neolithic, Jiang-Huai region (c. 3500 - 2200 BC)
Diameter, 16.6 cm; perforation diameter, 7.6 cm;
thickness, 0.4 - 0.8 cm

器表光素凸起，外侧边缘作齿牙状，内侧边缘较
锐利。此器与安徽凌家滩及南京营盘山等处所出
同类器相似。

鸟形佩
BIRD-SHAPED PENDANT

新石器时代 江淮地区（公元前3500～前2200年）
灰白玉 局部有沁
高 3.6、宽 7.4、厚 0.2 厘米

Neolithic, Jiang-Huai region (c. 3500 - 2200 BC)
Greyish-white jade with partial discoloration
Height, 3.6 cm; width, 7.4 cm ; thickness, 0.2 cm

作展翅状。平喙，以双面钻孔为眼，双翅外侧为
齿牙形。镂刻，背面有线性开料痕。已做二次琢
磨处理。此器物形制及制法与安徽薛家岗文化所
出同类器相似。

齿牙鱼形佩
FISH-SHAPED PENDANT

新石器时代 江淮地区（公元前3500～前2200年）
灰白玉 局部有沁
高4.1、宽12.5、厚0.2厘米

Neolithic, Jiang-Huai region (c. 3500 - 2200 BC)
Greyish-white jade with partial discoloration
Height, 4.1 cm; width, 12.5 cm; thickness, 0.2 cm

长条弧面体。上端平齐，左右两侧斜直有缺，作鱼
首状，圆形单钻孔为鱼眼。中部饰对称钩形缺。下
端为细齿牙状弧形边。此器的形制、制法与安徽
薛家岗文化中所出同类器相近。

虎首形璜
HUANG-SEGMENT WITH TIGER-HEAD-SHAPED ENDS

新石器时代　江淮地区（约公元前3500年～前2200年）
灰白玉　局部有沁
高3.0、长7.5、宽2.0、厚0.2～0.5厘米

Neolithic, Jiang-Huai region (c. 3500 - 2200 BC)
Greyish-white jade with partial discoloration
Height, 3.0; length, 7.5 cm; width, 2.0 cm;
thickness, 0.2 - 0.5 cm

扁圆弧形，两端为虎首状。立耳圆睛，前额凸起，挺鼻，以阴线刻画眼眶、胡须、鼻及前肢和爪，以双面偏心钻孔为睛。整器呈灰白色，器表润而有泽。此器造型与凌家滩1987年所出玉双虎首璜（87M8：26）极接近，唯璜身稍短，弧度较平。此类器还见于江淮地区其他同时期遗存中。其相对年代为江淮地区新石器晚期偏早阶段。

参见：
1.《故宫博物院藏文物珍品全集·玉器》上，图版17、第19页。商务印书馆（香港），1995年。
2.安徽省文物考古研究所《凌家滩玉器》，图版57、第59页，文、第128页。文物出版社，2000年。

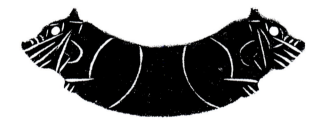

镯形器
BRACELET-SHAPED PENDANT

新石器时代 良渚文化（公元前3300～前2200年）
青灰玉 局部有沁
外径9.8、内径6.3、厚1.8厘米

Neolithic, Liangzhu culture (c. 3300 - 2200 BC)
Greyish-green jade with partial discoloration
Diameter, 9.8 cm; perforation diameter, 6.3 cm;
thickness, 1.8 cm

扁平环状。依其材质及形制，应为新石器时代良
渚文化遗物。

琮形器（2件）
TWO CONG-TUBES

新石器时代 良渚文化（公元前3300～前2200年）
青灰玉 有沁
高2.7、径1.3厘米（2件尺寸大致相同）

Neolithic, Liangzhu culture (c. 3300 - 2200 BC)
Greyish-green jade with partial discoloration
Height, 2.7 cm; diameter, 1.3 cm; two pieces similar in
size

体分三节，形制较小。良渚文化中期有类似造型的
小型玉琮出土。

管形琮
CYLINDRICAL CONG-TUBE

新石器时代 良渚文化（公元前3300～前2200年）
青玉 局部有沁
高9.3、上口径3.3～5.0、下口径3.2～4.4厘米

Neolithic, Liangzhu culture (c. 3300 - 2200 BC)
Green jade with partial discoloration
Height, 9.3 cm; diameter, 3.3 - 5.0 cm (top), 3.2 - 4.4 cm (bottom)

上宽下窄，器表饰三组简化兽面纹，各组间以凹阴线相隔。此器与良渚文化中晚期所出同类器相似。

虎首饰
TIGER-HEAD-SHAPED ORNAMENT

新石器时代 石家河文化（公元前2600～前2100年）
青玉
高2.5、宽6.3、厚2.1厘米

Neolithic, Shijiahe culture (c. 2600 - 2100 BC)
Green jade
Height, 2.5 cm; width, 6.3 cm; thickness, 2.1 cm

额中凸起，以多条短阴线表现眉。凸圆睛，宽鼻
有须。透雕长方口，有齿，下腭处有残缺。额两
侧雕虎耳。器两侧钻有不规则形贯穿孔。此件虎
首饰与湖北肖家屋脊所出虎头（M71：6）风格接
近，与肖家屋脊标本010及上海博物馆藏石家河
文化虎头饰相似。

参见：
1.湖北省博物馆、湖北省文物考古研究所、北京大学考古学系
《肖家屋脊》，文、第325页，图256、257，彩版10：3、11：1。
文物出版社，1999年。
2.上海博物馆《中国古代玉器馆》，第9页。

双孔钺
YUE-CEREMONIAL BLADE

新石器时代 龙山文化（公元前2800～前2100年）
青玉 局部有沁
高16.2、上宽7.2、下宽8.6、厚0.3～0.6厘米

Neolithic, Longshan culture (c. 2800 - 2100 BC)
Green jade with partial discoloration
Height, 16.2 cm; width 7.2 cm (top), 8.6 cm (bottom);
thickness, 0.3 - 0.6 cm

上端平直稍厚，刃部略宽微作弧形。薄刃，刃口
两侧一边竖直，一边向外斜出。当为黄河流域龙
山文化中晚期遗物。

兽面纹琮
CONG-TUBE WITH ANIMAL MASK DESIGN

新石器时代 陕西地区（公元前2300～前2000年）
青玉 半透明 器表有数处条状沁斑
高7.3、上口7.4～8.3、下口7.3～8.2厘米

Neolithic, Shaanxi region (c. 2300 - 2000 BC)
Translucent green jade with some discolored streaks
Height, 7.3 cm; diameter, 7.4 - 8.3 cm (top), 7.3 - 8.2
cm (bottom)

器表饰四组双层兽面纹，饰纹以减地凸起阴线为
主，器表抛光。形制与陕西延安碾庄芦山卯采集
的玉琮相近，当属龙山文化遗存。此器在两组兽
面之间有宋人所刻内插花枝的瓶状标识，当传世
已久。

参见：
中国玉器全集编辑委员会《中国玉器全集》（1）原始社会，图
版5、第5页，文、第231页。河北美术出版社，1992年。

龙形璜
DRAGON-SHAPED *HUANG*-SEGMENT

商晚期（公元前 1300～前 1046 年）
白玉 半透明
长 8.5、宽 1.2、厚 0.4 厘米

Late Shang (c. 1300 - 1046 BC)
Translucent white jade
Length, 8.5 cm; width, 1.2 cm; thickness, 0.4 cm

夔龙形。斜角臣字目，宝瓶角。曲肢，卷尾，尾后
光素有刃。玉质润白细腻，系上好的和阗玉。此器
为商晚期玉器中少见的珍品。

虎
TIGER PENDANT

商晚期（公元前 1300～前 1046 年）
青玉　半透明
高 2.4、长 7.2、厚 0.5 厘米

Late Shang (c. 1300 - 1046 BC)
Translucent green jade
Height, 2.4 cm; length, 7.2 cm; thickness, 0.5 cm

双面纹饰同。虎首微垂，大斜角臣字目，张口露
齿，云耳。双肢曲而伏地，爪分双趾，粗长尾回
卷上扬。虎身饰大斜刀回纹，口内及尾部有孔。为
商晚期常见之物。

回首虎形佩
TIGER WITH BACK-TURNED HEAD

商晚期（公元前 1300～前 1046 年）
青玉　半透明　局部有沁
高 4.0、长 6.2、厚 0.5 厘米

Late Shang (c. 1300 - 1046 BC)
Translucent green jade with partial discoloration
Height, 4.0 cm; length, 6.2 cm; thickness, 0.5 cm

回首，菱形目，宝瓶状角，张口利齿。屈体，卷尾，
尾后有条状有刃刻刀。为商晚期之物。

参见：
《故宫博物院藏文物珍品全集·玉器》上，图版 70、第 83 页。
商务印书馆（香港），1995 年。

曲颈鹤
CRANE WITH BENT NECK

商晚期（公元前 1300～前 1046 年）
青玉
高 10.0、宽 6.0、厚 0.6 厘米

Late Shang (c. 1300 - 1046 BC)
Green jade
Height, 10.0 cm; width, 6.0 cm; thickness, 0.6 cm

双面纹饰同。曲颈，俯首，敛翅，垂尾，立爪。眼
作圆孔。与河南安阳殷墟妇好墓所出一对长颈鹤
形制相同，为商晚期玉作精品。

参见：
1.《殷墟玉器》图版 48，器 437、416。文物出版社，1982 年。
2.《殷墟妇好墓》，图 87：14、16，文、第 163 页，彩版 33：2，
图版 145：4。文物出版社，1980 年。

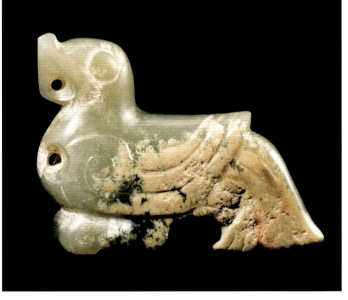

曲颈鸟
BIRD WITH BENT NECK

商晚期（公元前 1300～前 1046 年）
青玉 局部有沁
高 3.2、长 3.8、厚 0.9 厘米

Late Shang (c. 1300 - 1046 BC)
Green jade with partial discoloration
Height, 3.2 cm; length, 3.8 cm; thickness, 0.9 cm

圆睛尖喙，曲颈弓背，爪前伸，尾垂地。依其形
制，当为商晚期遗物。

钩喙鸟
BIRD WITH HOOKED BEAK

商晚期（公元前 1300～前 1046 年）
青玉 局部有沁
高 4.0、长 4.5、厚 1.1 厘米

Late Shang (c. 1300 - 1046 BC)
Green jade with partial discoloration
Height, 4.0 cm; length, 4.5 cm; thickness, 1.1 cm

钩喙，凸圆睛，单爪前伏，宽尾垂地。喙部及前
胸处有圆穿。此器同河南安阳殷墟西区 M53 所出
玉鸟（M53：4）极接近，同类器还见于殷墟中小
型墓及山东滕县前掌大等同期遗存中，为商晚期
常见器物。

参见：
《殷墟玉器》图版 53：左。文物出版社，1982 年。

高冠鹦鹉
PARROT WITH TALL CREST

商晚期（公元前 1300～前 1046 年）
青玉　半透明　局部有沁
高 9.3、宽 3.2、厚 0.4 厘米

Late Shang (c. 1300 - 1046 BC)
Translucent green jade with partial discoloration
Height, 9.3 cm; width, 3.2 cm; thickness, 0.4 cm

双面纹饰相同。侧身屈体，头上有双戈形高冠，凸
额阔嘴，方圆睛，脑后有飞羽，敛翅卷尾。足下
有短榫，嘴部有双面钻孔供佩系。造型为殷商晚
期所习见。

参见：
Alfred Salmony, Carved Jade of Ancient China
Reprinted by Han-Shan Tang 1982, Plate XV III, 1.

蝉纹玉勒
LE-TUBE WITH CICADA DESIGN

商晚期（公元前 1300～前 1046 年）
青玉 半透明
高 1.9、长 4.0 厘米

Late Shang (c. 1300 - 1046 BC)
Translucent green jade
Height, 1.9 cm; length, 4.0 cm

管状。器表以单阴线刻首、翅，无睛，无口，吻
下为斜面，体有对钻的贯穿孔。

蝉纹玉勒
LE-TUBE WITH CICADA DESIGN

商晚期（公元前 1300～前 1046 年）
青玉 局部有棕红黑沁
高 2.2、长 4.0 厘米

Late Shang (c. 1300 - 1046 BC)
Green jade with brownish-red and black suffusion in
places
Height, 2.2 cm; length, 4.0 cm

器表呈黄绿色，束腰扁圆体，中空，有对钻横贯
孔。两端双面各饰减地浮雕蝉纹。器表润而光泽。
蝉纹的表现手法与江西新干大洋州商代墓葬所出
圆形坠饰的蝉纹相似。

参见：
江西省文物考古研究所、江西省博物馆、新干县博物馆《新干
商代大墓》，文物出版社，1997 年。

平冠侧身人形佩
HUMAN FIGURE IN PROFILE WITH FLAT HAT

商晚期（公元前 1300～前 1046 年）
松石 局部沁蚀
高 6.2、宽 2.4、厚 1.0 厘米

Late Shang (c. 1300 - 1046 BC)
Turquoise with partial discoloration
Height, 6.2 cm; width, 2.4 cm; thickness, 1.0 cm

双面纹饰同。平冠，臣字目，云形耳，宽鼻。臀
部双面均有"⊕"形标识，下部有短榫，榫下有双
面钻孔。造型同中国国家博物馆藏商代晚期玉人
相近，但后者为高冠。此件器物形神俱佳，为难
得一见的松石精品。

参见：
1.中国玉器全集编辑委员会《中国玉器全集》(2) 商·西周，图
版 177、第 128 页，文、第 278 页。河北美术出版社，1993 年。
2.商志䪭《论虢国墓中之商代玉器及其它》，见香港中文大学中
国考古艺术研究中心《东亚玉器》Ⅱ，图 41.2.2，第 32 页。香
港中文大学，1998 年。该器出土于河南三门峡虢国墓地 M2009，
制作年代为商代晚期。

熊首人身佩
PENDANT OF BEAR HEAD ON HUMAN BODY

商晚期（公元前 1300～前 1046 年）
松石 局部有沁蚀
高 4.2、宽 2.6、厚 1.0 厘米

Late Shang (c. 1300 - 1046 BC)
Turquoise with partial discoloration
Height, 4.2 cm; width, 2.6 cm; thickness, 1.0 cm

双面纹饰同。直立，短耳，臣字目，双手并指抚
膝，踞坐。左侧扉棱上有双面钻系孔。此器为殷
商时期松石珍品，与妇好墓所出玉熊有相似之
处，唯质地不同。

参见：
1.叶义《中国玉雕》图24、第60～61页。香港艺术馆，1982年。
2.中国玉器全集编辑委员会《中国玉器全集》(2)商·西周，图
版70、第58页，文、第23页。河北美术出版社，1994年（香
港版）。

高冠鹦鹉
PARROT WITH TALL CREST

商晚期（公元前 1300～前 1046 年）
松石 下部有沁
高 6.7、宽 3.0、厚 0.6 厘米

Late Shang (c. 1300 - 1046 BC)
Turquoise with discoloration on lower part
Height, 6.7 cm; width, 3.0 cm; thickness, 0.6 cm

双面纹饰同。一侧冠部、胸部及尾外侧有钮牙饰。
钩喙，高冠，挺胸，卷尾。此器与河南安阳殷墟
妇好墓所出 325 号玉鹦鹉相近，神形俱佳，为难
得一见的松石珍品。

参见：
中国社会科学院考古研究所《殷墟玉器》图版 47。文物出版社，
1982 年。

回首虎形佩
TIGER WITH BACK-TURNED HEAD

商晚期（公元前 1300～前 1046 年）
松石 局部有黑灰斑
高 3.8、长 6.3、厚 0.3 厘米

Late Shang (c. 1300 - 1046 BC)
Turquoise with blackish-grey patches
Height, 3.8 cm; length, 6.3 cm; thickness, 0.3 cm

作回首曲体卷尾状。椭圆目，柱形角，张口露齿，
单爪前屈。胸前有对钻圆孔，尾部有条状薄刃外
凸，口部以多次管钻法刻成牙齿，乃殷人典型手
法。此器与北京故宫博物院藏玉龙形小刀极似。

参见：
《故宫博物院藏文物珍品全集·玉器》上，图版 70、第 83 页。
商务印书馆（香港），1995 年。

刻铭玉璧
BI-DISK WITH INSCRIPTIONS

商末（公元前 1112～前 1046 年）
青玉
外径 3.4、内径 0.4、厚 0.9 厘米

Ending period of Shang (c. 1112 - 1046 BC)
Green jade
Diameter, 3.4 cm; perforation diameter, 0.4 cm;
thickness, 0.9 cm

此璧虽小，但璧肉右侧环刻"壬辰妬易燕"五字，刻铭笔划微小纤细。经著名学者李学勤先生考证，此璧当是商元文丁、帝乙、帝辛三世间某王后赐于名"燕"的女子的。商代刻铭玉器存世不多，属商末时期的更少，此璧系商末三世时期六十七年间某王后赐下，为此则尤显重要。

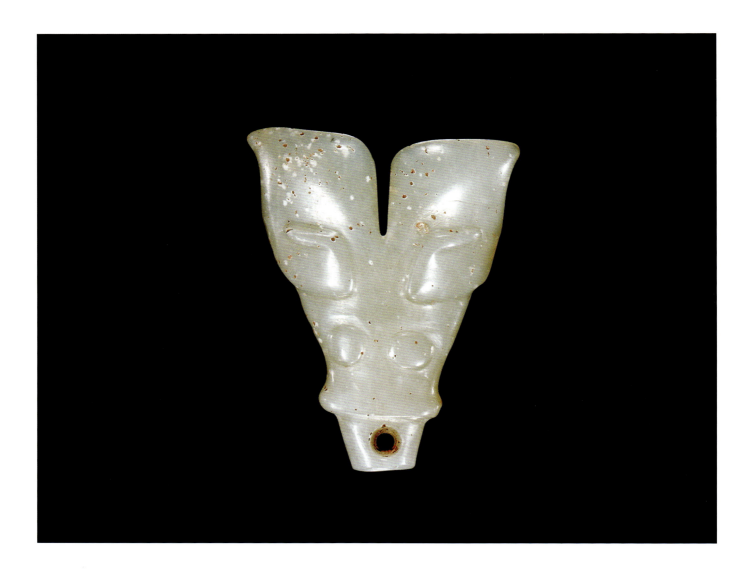

兽面饰
ANIMAL-FACE FITTING

商末（公元前1100～前1046年）
青白玉 半透明
高4.0、宽3.1、厚0.5厘米

Ending period of Shang (c. 1100 - 1046 BC)
Translucent pale green jade
Height, 4.0 cm; width, 3.1 cm; thickness, 0.5 cm

双角叉分高耸，凸圆睛，阔嘴。嘴下斜收短榫，榫
上有单面钻圆孔。背面光素作环形内凹。从其形
制看，应是作镶嵌件使用。从时代看，当属商代
末期。

参见：
傅熹年《古玉缀英》，图33、第72页，文、第73页。中华书局
（香港），1995年。

戚
QI-AXE

西周（公元前 1046～前 771 年）
青玉 局部有沁
高 4.0、宽 3.0、厚 0.6 厘米

Western Zhou (c. 1046 - 771 BC)
Green jade with partial discoloration
Height, 4.0 cm; width, 3.0 cm; thickness, 0.6 cm

上端平齐较厚，两侧有钮牙饰，下端为斜弧薄刃。

侧身人龙合雕佩
PENDANT OF HUMAN-DRAGON HYBRID IN PROFILE

西周（公元前 1046～前 771 年）
青玉 半透明 局部有灰白沁
高 7.4、宽 2.4、厚 0.3 厘米

Western Zhou (c. 1046 - 771 BC)
Translucent green jade with greyish-white suffusion in places
Height, 7.4 cm; width, 2.4 cm; thickness, 0.3 cm

双面纹饰同，器表多朱砂痕。侧身曲肢蹲踞。棱形目、粗眉、高鼻、小嘴、云耳。首上蜷伏一回首张口、曲肢侧身的龙。胸部为一俯视的曲体龙。部分镂雕，首及臀部有单面钻圆孔。此佩人龙合体，制作精美，为西周时期贵族所用。此器与北京故宫博物院藏玉镂雕人首龙形佩及河南三门峡虢国墓地 M2001、M2009 所出同类器多有近似之处。

参见：
1.中国玉器全集编辑委员会《中国玉器全集》(2) 商·西周，图版 223、第 162 页，文、第 293 页。河北美术出版社，1994 年（香港版）
2.河南省文物考古研究所、三门峡市文物工作队：姜涛、王龙正等《三门峡虢国墓》第一卷（上），人形佩（M2011：452），图二五三：15、16，第 360 页，文、第 362 页下，彩版三十九：2，图版 134：1，文物出版社，1999 年。

侧身人龙合雕佩
PENDANT OF HUMAN-DRAGON HYBRID IN PROFILE

西周（公元前 1046～前 771 年）
青白玉 局部有棕色沁
高 7.7、宽 2.4、厚 0.5 厘米

Western Zhou (c. 1046 - 771 BC)
Translucent pale green jade with brown suffusion in places
Height, 7.7 cm; width, 2.4 cm; thickness, 0.5 cm

双面纹饰同。主体为一侧身蹲踞之人，着平冠，双睛，隆鼻，小嘴，云耳，卷尾。颈后为一俯视的龙，龙尾卷于冠上。胸部及足部亦为俯视龙形。颈后有单面圆孔，供佩系之用。此器造型、纹饰及做工为西周中晚期常见，与北京故宫博物院藏镂雕人形佩极似。

参见：
1.《故宫博物院藏文物珍品全集·玉器》上，图版102、第122页。商务印书馆（香港），1995年。
2.中国玉器全集编辑委员会《中国玉器全集》(2) 商·西周，图版 223、第162页，文、第293页。河北美术出版社，1994年（香港版）。
3.河南省文物考古研究所、三门峡市文物工作队：姜涛、王龙正等《三门峡虢国墓》第一卷（上），人形佩 (M2011:452)，图二五三：15、16，第360页，文、第362页下，彩版三九：2，图版一三四：1。文物出版社，1999年。

人龙合雕佩
PENDANT OF HUMAN-DRAGON HYBRID

西周（公元前 1046～前 771 年）
青玉 局部有沁
高 5.5、宽 5.5、厚 0.4 厘米

Western Zhou (c. 1046 - 771 BC)
Green jade with partial discoloration
Height, 5.5 cm; width, 5.5 cm; thickness, 0.4 cm

正面略鼓，背面稍凹，器中部有圆穿，单面施纹。
器身一端为人首，另端为卷鼻吐舌的龙首。此类
构图与纹样常见于西周晚期、两周之际，如河南
三门峡虢国墓地、山西侯马晋侯墓地等处。此类
佩饰多用于高等级组佩之中，如组合项饰于颈后
的结合处。

人龙合纹佩
PENDANT WITH HUMAN-DRAGON HYBRID
DESIGN

西周（公元前 1046～前 771 年）
白玉 半透明
高 4.1、宽 5.2、厚 0.3 厘米

Western Zhou (c. 1046 - 771 BC)
Translucent white jade
Height, 4.1 cm; width, 5.2 cm; thickness, 0.3 cm

双面施纹。器形主体为双体连首的龙形，龙首分
饰于两端。一侧龙首獠牙末端有一回首侧视的人
首，上端及右侧伏卧一回首的龙形。人龙合雕、人
龙合纹的构图及表现手法是西周晚期玉作的一大
特点。此器与河南新郑唐户 11 号西周墓所出的一
件同类器几乎相同。

衔尾龙形佩
COILED DRAGON WITH TAIL IN MOUTH

西周（公元前1046～前771年）
青白玉 半透明 局部有沁
径4.2、厚0.4厘米

Western Zhou (c. 1046 - 771 BC)
Translucent pale green jade with partial discoloration
Diameter, 4.2 cm; thickness, 0.4 cm

双面纹饰同。曲体团身，张口衔尾，龙角后伏，臣
字目。体饰重环纹，尾施卷云纹。下腭处有一单
孔供佩系。造型及纹饰与河南三门峡虢国墓
M2009所出同类器极为相近，为西周晚期典型器。

圆形龙纹佩
ROUND PENDANT WITH DRAGON DESIGN

西周（公元前 1046～前 771 年）
青白玉 半透明
径 3.7、厚 1.0 厘米

Western Zhou (c. 1046 - 771 BC)
Translucent pale green jade
Diameter, 3.7 cm; thickness, 1.0 cm

正面隆起作弧面，背面平直。正面为两条相互盘绕
的龙，背面为单龙，龙身均施重环纹。此器构图、
做工均佳，原器主当为西周晚期的高等级贵族。

参见：
傅熹年《古玉掇英》雕鸟纹涡纹圆饰片，图 59、第 103 页。中华
书局（香港），1995 年。

缠体人首纹璜
DRAGON *HUANG*-SEGMENT WITH HUMAN-HEAD
DESIGN AT ENDS

西周（公元前 1046～前 771 年）
青玉 半透明
长 9.9、宽 1.7、厚 0.5 厘米

Western Zhou (c. 1046 - 771 BC)
Translucent green jade
Length, 9.9 cm; width, 1.7 cm; thickness, 0.5 cm

玉质细润，双面纹饰同。器表饰缠体人首龙身纹。
两端饰有冠人首纹，人首作圆眼阔嘴侧视状。尾
回卷处各雕一小龙首。身饰重环纹。造型及纹饰
流行于西周中晚期。

曲体龙形佩
PENDANT OF CURVED DRAGON

西周（公元前 1046～前 771 年）
青玉 半透明
高 4.2、长 4.7、厚 0.4 厘米

Western Zhou (c. 1046 - 771 BC)
Translucent green jade
Height, 4.2 cm; length, 4.7 cm; thickness, 0.4 cm

双面纹饰同。一侧龙首稍大，阔口，长舌回卷，舌
面为一简化龙首。躯干后部为一无下腭之小龙
首。龙尾回翻，一面尾部有线性开料痕。

兽面纹佩
PENDANT WITH ANIMAL FACE DESIGN

西周（公元前 1046～前 771 年）
青玉 局部有沁
高 2.7、上宽 3.5、下宽 2.5、厚 0.6 厘米

Western Zhou (c. 1046 - 771 BC)
Green jade with partial discoloration
Height, 2.7 cm; width, 3.5 cm (top), 2.5 cm (bottom);
thickness, 0.6 cm

双面施纹，中部有单面钻孔。器表所饰兽面纹常
见于西周中晚期，如河南三门峡虢国墓曾出土数
件与之相同者。此器当时应是作为镶嵌之用。

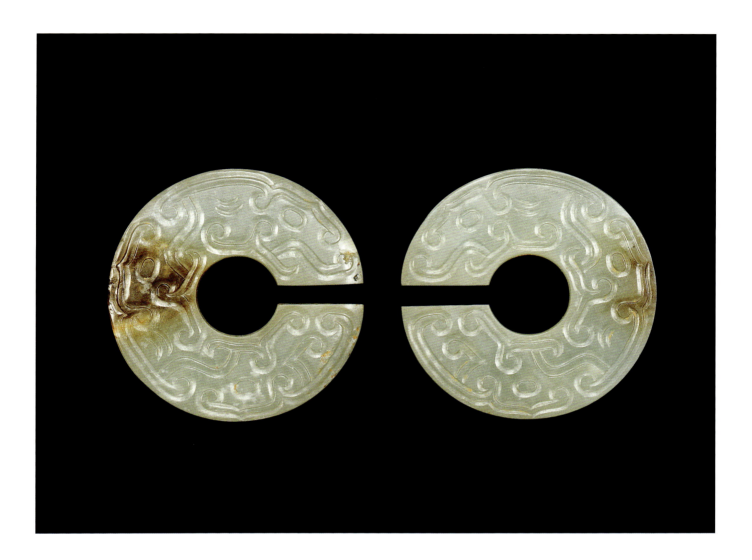

龙首纹玦（1对）
PAIR OF *JUE*-SLIT DISKS WITH DRAGON HEAD DESIGN

西周（公元前 1046～前 771 年）
白玉 半透明 局部有沁
直径 3.8、厚 0.4 厘米

Western Zhou (c. 1046 - 771 BC)
Translucent white jade with partial discoloration
Diameter, 3.8 cm; thickness, 0.4 cm

单面施纹，纹饰为三联龙首。龙首作椭圆目、吐舌状，并以上翘之舌与前面的龙首相联。玦为西周时期常见之器，但三联龙首纹则少见。

高冠鸟形佩 (1 对)
PAIR OF BIRDS WITH TALL CRESTS

西周 (公元前 1046～前 771 年)
青玉 半透明 局部有沁
高 4.4、宽 2.4、上端厚 0.5、下端厚 0.3 厘米

Western Zhou (c. 1046 - 771 BC)
Translucent green jade with partial discoloration
Height, 4.4 cm; width, 2.4 cm; thickness, 0.5 cm (top),
0.3 cm (bottom)

单面施纹。长翎后披, 凸额圆睛, 扁阔嘴, 曲体。
首上有单钻圆孔, 下部有对钻圆孔, 体侧有扉棱。
此类扉棱见于西周时期, 扉棱的做法与1978年西
安长安县配件厂所出鸟纹璜相近, 圆睛扁嘴的表
现方式与1981年出土于西安沣西的鸟形佩 (原称
玉虎纹璜) 相同。

鱼形璜
FISH *HUANG*-SEGMENT

西周（公元前 1046～前 771 年）
青玉 局部有沁
长 8.0、宽 2.3、厚 0.3 厘米

Western Zhou (c. 1046 - 771 BC)
Green jade with partial discoloration
Length, 8.0 cm; width, 2.3 cm; thickness, 0.3 cm

双面施纹。阴线刻圆眼、腮、背鳍、腹鳍、尾及
鳞纹。首尾处各有一圆穿。此类器西周晚期常见。

参见：
河南省文物考古研究所、三门峡市文物工作队《上村岭虢国墓
地 M2006 的清理》，3 式鱼形璜（M2006：91、116），图二九、图
三一、第 17 页，图三八：5、7，第 19 页，文、第 10、11 页。
《文物》，1995 年第 1 期。

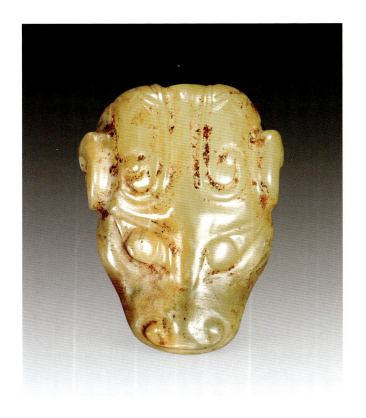

圆雕鸟形佩
BIRD FIGURE

西周（公元前 1046～前 771 年）
青玉 有沁
高 5.4、宽 3.1、厚 0.3～1.5 厘米

Western Zhou(c. 1046 - 771 BC)
Green jade with partial discoloration
Height, 5.4 cm; width, 3.1 cm; thickness, 0.3 - 1.5 cm

圆首，尖嘴，双晴，敛翅分尾。背面有穿及供镶
嵌用的斜面台阶形榫。此类鸟形佩最早出现于商
晚期，流行于整个西周时期。

参见：
傅熹年《古玉掇英》，插图二十九、三十、第 42、43 页。中华书
局（香港），1995 年。

牛首形佩
BULL HEAD PENDANT

西周（公元前 1046～前 771 年）
青白玉 半透明
高 3.5、宽 2.4、厚 0.9 厘米

Western Zhou (c. 1046 - 771 BC)
Translucent pale green jade
Height, 3.5 cm; width, 2.4 cm; thickness, 0.9 cm

凸晴，臣字目，盘角，阔鼻，扁口，额后有竖向
对钻斜穿，背部平素。此类半圆雕玉作，除供佩
系外也可用作镶嵌。

鱼形璜
FISH *HUANG*-SEGMENT

西周（公元前1046～前771年）
青玉　局部有沁
长8.0、宽2.3、厚0.3厘米

Western Zhou (c. 1046 - 771 BC)
Green jade with partial discoloration
Length, 8.0 cm; width, 2.3 cm; thickness, 0.3 cm

双面施纹。阴线刻圆眼、腮、背鳍、腹鳍、尾及
鳞纹。首尾处各有一圆穿。此类器西周晚期常见。

参见：
河南省文物考古研究所、三门峡市文物工作队《上村岭虢国墓
地M2006的清理》，3式鱼形璜（M2006：91、116），图二九、图
三一、第17页，图三八：5、7，第13页，文、第10、11页。
《文物》，1995年第1期。

鱼形璜
FISH *HUANG*-SEGMENT

西周（公元前 1046～前 771 年）
青白玉
高 2.8、长 5.3、厚 0.5 厘米

Western Zhou (c. 1046 - 771 BC)
Pale green jade
Height, 2.8 cm; length, 5.3 cm; thickness, 0.5 cm

双面施纹。尖唇，圆睛，躬身，尾分双杈。口及
尾处各有一双面钻圆孔。西周晚期器物。

圆雕犀牛
RHINOCEROS FIGURE

西周（公元前 1046～前 771 年)
青玉 局部有沁
高 3.8、长 7.1 厘米

Western Zhou (c. 1046 - 771 BC)
Green jade with partial discoloration
Height, 3.8 cm; length, 7.1 cm

隆鼻大耳，探首前视。塌腰耸臀，短尾。四足斜
立向前，有蹄。西周时期的圆雕动物类玉作极少，
此件依制作工艺，当为西周晚期之物。

圆雕鸟形佩
BIRD FIGURE

西周（公元前 1046～前 771 年）
青玉　有沁
高 5.4、宽 3.1、厚 0.3～1.5 厘米

Western Zhou(c. 1046 - 771 BC)
Green jade with partial discoloration
Height, 5.4 cm; width, 3.1 cm; thickness, 0.3 - 1.5 cm

圆首，尖嘴，双睛，敛翅分尾。背面有穿及供镶
嵌用的斜面台阶形榫。此类鸟形佩最早出现于商
晚期，流行于整个西周时期。

参见：
傅熹年《古玉掇英》，插图二十九、三十、第 42、43 页。中华书
局（香港），1995 年。

牛首形佩
BULL HEAD PENDANT

西周（公元前 1046～前 771 年）
青白玉　半透明
高 3.5、宽 2.4、厚 0.9 厘米

Western Zhou (c. 1046 - 771 BC)
Translucent pale green jade
Height, 3.5 cm; width, 2.4 cm; thickness, 0.9 cm

凸睛，臣字目，盘角，阔鼻，扁口，额后有竖向
对钻斜穿，背部平素。此类半圆雕玉作，除供佩
系外也可用作镶嵌。

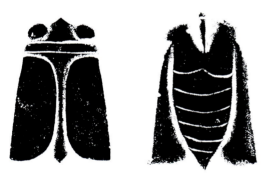

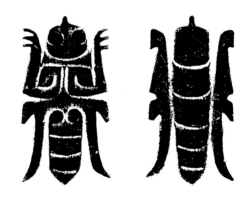

蝉形佩
CICADA FIGURE

西周（公元前 1046～前 771 年）
青白玉　半透明
高 4.1、宽 2.5、厚 0.8 厘米

Western Zhou (c. 1046 - 771 BC)
Translucent pale green jade
Height, 4.1 cm; width, 2.5 cm; thickness, 0.8 cm

凸睛敛翼，背面腹部施六道阴线，吻下有一对钻
横穿圆孔。造型简练，生动传神。

参见：
《中国肖生玉雕》，图版 33、第 66、67 页。香港艺术馆，1996 年。

曲肢蝉形佩
PENDANT OF LEG-BENT CICADA

西周（公元前 1046～前 771 年）
青玉　半透明
高 4.7、宽 2.4、厚 0.3 厘米

Western Zhou (c. 1046 - 771 BC)
Translucent green jade
Height, 4.7 cm; width, 2.4 cm; thickness, 0.3 cm

尖嘴，凸圆睛。双肢屈而前伸，翅分两侧略外张。
以宽阴线刻出腹部，背面以阴线示首、腹。造型
与表现手法为西周晚期习见。

凤鸟纹箍形器
TUBE WITH PHOENIX DESIGN

西周（公元前1046～前771年）
青褐玉　半透明
高7.0、外径6.2～7.0、厚0.8厘米

Western Zhou (c. 1046 - 771 BC)
Translucent brownish-green jade
Height, 7.0 cm; diameter, 6.2 - 7.0 cm; tube-wall
thickness, 0.8 cm

圆筒形，上宽下窄。纹饰主题为四组两两相背而
立的凤鸟纹。凤鸟纹上下以减地突起双阳线为
边，并界出光素宽栏。上端又饰有蕉叶纹一周。下
端两侧各有一处凹进的小缺。此器原应是镶于他
物之上的。

兽面形饰
ANIMAL FACE PLAQUE

春秋（公元前 770～前 476 年）
青玉 半透明
高 4.5、上宽 5.0、下宽 3.1、厚 0.6 厘米

Spring and Autumn Period (c. 770 - 476 BC)
Translucent green jade
Height, 4.5 cm; width, 5.0 cm (top), 3.1 cm (bottom);
thickness, 0.6 cm

器作扁平状，上宽下窄。兽面形，双面施纹。中部以一条横向单阴线为界，下部刻眉、目、鼻、口、须、角等，上部以双阴线刻出云纹、圆圈纹等，花纹繁缛。中部偏上有一不规则"十"字形穿，上部左右有半圆形穿，上端正中偏下处有一小圆穿。同类器常见于春秋时期，如河南光山宝相寺黄君孟夫妇合葬墓及淅川下寺 M1 所出玉牌。

参见：
1. 河南信阳地区文管会、光山县文管会《春秋早期黄君孟夫妇墓发掘报告》，《考古》，1984 年第 4 期。
2. 河南省文物研究所、河南省丹江库区考古发掘队、淅川县博物馆《淅川下寺春秋楚墓》，图版三九：1、图八二：1、2、第 100 页，文、第 98 页。文物出版社，1991 年。

龙形佩
DRAGON SHAPED PENDANT

春秋（公元前 770～前 476 年）
青玉 半透明
高 8.0、厚 0.5 厘米

Spring and Autumn Period (c. 770 - 476 BC)
Translucent green jade
Height, 8.0 cm; thickness, 0.5 cm

双面施纹。张口吐舌，长舌方折向上，与鼻平齐。
曲体呈"C"形，通体饰变形勾连云纹。龙口内及
身上部有圆穿。此器与台湾蓝田山房所藏的两件龙
纹佩极相似。依形制及工艺，当属春秋晚期器物。

参见：
邓淑萍《蓝田山房藏玉百选》，龙纹佩，图 54、第 184 页。台湾
财团法人年喜文教基金会，1995 年。

弧面回首虎形饰
CURVED TIGER ORNAMENT WITH BACK-TURNED
HEAD

春秋（公元前 770～前 476 年）
青玉 器表有灰黑棕红沁
长 7.1、厚 0.4 厘米

Spring and Autumn Period (c. 770 - 476 BC)
Green jade with greyish-black and brownish-red
suffusion
Length, 7.1 cm; thickness, 0.4 cm

半圆弧形。虎作回首屈体、卷尾蹲伏状。虎目椭
圆，耳上竖，张口，上腭外卷，四肢屈而蹲伏，背
负高浮雕披鬣。器表满饰凸起勾云纹，颈部有钻
孔。整器做工甚精，为春秋晚期器物。

回首虎形佩
TIGER PENDANT WITH BACK-TURNED HEAD

春秋（公元前770～前476年）
青玉　局部有棕红沁
高2.9、长5.2、厚0.4厘米

Spring and Autumn Period (c. 770 - 476 BC)
Green jade with brownish-red suffusion in places
Height, 2.9 cm; length, 5.2 cm; thickness, 0.4 cm

曲颈回首，突睛圆目，塌腰耸臀，四肢前伏，尾上扬。身饰勾云纹，足上为细鳞纹，刻画细致。时代当为春秋晚期。此类造型的虎曾见于河南淅川下寺3号墓，但下寺3号墓的虎（原报告称玉兽）为阴线饰纹。

参见：
中国玉器全集编辑委员会《中国玉器全集》(3)春秋·战国，图版79、第48页，文、第229页。河北美术出版社，1993年。

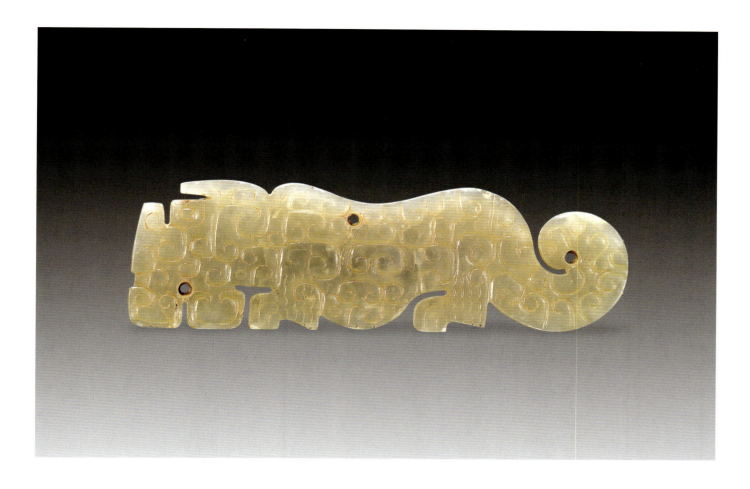

虎形佩
TIGER SHAPED PENDANT

春秋（公元前 770～前 476 年）
青白玉　半透明
高 2.6、长 8.2、厚 0.2 厘米

Spring and Autumn Period (c. 770 - 476 BC)
Translucent pale green jade
Height, 2.6 cm; length, 8.2 cm; thickness, 0.2 cm

扁平体，双面饰纹同。屈肢俯首，口微张，凹腰
凸腹，双足前伸作卧伏状，虎尾上扬回卷。虎身
满饰勾云纹及并行线纹。口、背、尾部各有小孔，
以供佩系。此器与河南淅川下寺 3 号墓所出几乎
相同，为流行于春秋晚期的标准器。

参见：

1. 河南省文物研究所、河南省丹江库区考古发掘队、淅川县博
物馆《淅川下寺春秋楚墓》，图版八七：2、图一七六：4、第 237
页，文，第 236 页。文物出版社，1991 年。

2. 中国玉器全集编辑委员会《中国玉器全集》(3) 春秋·战国，
图版 87、第 52 页，文、第 231 页。河北美术出版社，1993 年。

管形龙纹玦（1对）
PAIR OF *JUE*-SLIT TUBES WITH DRAGON DESIGN

春秋（公元前770～前476年）
青玉 半透明
高3.1、上端径2.3、下端径2.4、厚0.6厘米

Spring and Autumn Period (c. 770 - 476 BC)
Translucent green jade
Height, 3.1 cm; diameter, 2.3 cm (top); 2.4 cm (bottom);
thickness, 0.6 cm

柱形管状，一侧有竖直缺。器身饰六组对角相向
的屈体龙纹，上下两端饰勾云纹。此器造型与河
南信阳光山县宝相寺黄君孟夫妇墓所出极为相
似；与稍晚于前者、传为河南新郑李家楼所出的
两件管形龙玦也多有相似之处。此两件管形龙纹
玦为春秋早中期少见的精品。

参见：
1.中国玉器全集编辑委员会《中国玉器全集》(3)春秋·战国，
图版6、第5页，文、第202页。河北美术出版社，1993年。
2.林淑心《中国古代玉器》，图34～36。台湾历史博物馆，台
北，1981年。

柱形龙首纹饰（1 对）
PAIR OF CYLINDERS WITH DRAGON HEAD DE-
SIGN

春秋（公元前 770～前 476 年）
青白玉 半透明 局部有沁
高 2.6、上端径 2.0、下端径 1.8 厘米

Spring and Autumn Period (c. 770 - 476 BC)
Translucent pale green jade with partial discoloration
Height, 2.6 cm; diameter, 2.0 cm (top), 1.8 cm (bottom)

柱状，通体饰隐起的龙首纹，上下端饰圆形勾云
纹。其造型、纹饰颇似 1988 年山西太原金胜村晋
卿赵氏墓所出者。

参见：
中国玉器全集编辑委员会《中国玉器全集》(3) 春秋·战国，图
版五三、第 34 页，文、第 219 页。河北美术出版社，1993 年。

管形龙首纹饰
OVAL TUBE WITH DRAGON HEAD DESIGN

春秋（公元前 770～前 476 年）
白玉 半透明 局部有沁
高 2.8、外径 1.2～1.6、内径 0.5 厘米

Spring and Autumn Period (c. 770 - 476 BC)
Translucent white jade with partial discoloration
Height, 2.8 cm; diameter, 1.2 - 1.6 cm; perforation
diameter, 0.5 cm

扁圆管形。上、下端分别以宽条状斜线纹为栏，通
体满饰凸起的变形龙纹，做工精细规整。此形制
玉饰流行于春秋中晚期，但白玉质地的较为少见。

龙纹管形饰
OVAL TUBE WITH DRAGON DESIGN

春秋（公元前 770～前 476 年）
白玉 半透明 局部有沁
高 5.5、宽 1.2、厚 0.8 厘米

Spring and Autumn Period (c. 770 - 476 BC)
Translucent white jade with partial discoloration
Height, 5.5 cm; width, 1.2 cm; thickness, 0.8 cm

长条扁管状。器表上下端以带状斜线纹为栏，栏
下为一周卷云纹。其间满饰四栏共十二条凸起的
变形龙纹。玉质晶莹润泽，纹饰布局繁缛，当为
春秋中晚期高等级贵族用物。

龙首纹玦(1 对)
PAIR OF *JUE*-SLIT DISKS WITH DRAGON DESIGN

春秋（公元前770～前476年）
青玉 半透明
外径5.4、内径1.2、厚0.2厘米

Spring and Autumn Period (c. 770 - 476 BC)
Translucent green jade
Diameter, 5.4 cm; perforation diameter, 1.2 cm;
thickness, 0.2 cm

双面饰纹同。纹饰主体为两两相对的四个龙首
纹，龙首间填以勾云纹。做工规整，所饰纹饰流
行于春秋中晚期。此两件玦与河南淅川下寺M7所
出多有近似。

参见：

1.河南省文物研究所、河南省丹江库区考古发掘队、淅川县博
物馆《淅川下寺春秋楚墓》，图版一五：1，文、第38页。文物
出版社，1991年。

兽面纹拱形饰
ARC-SHAPED ORNAMENT WITH ANIMAL FACE DESIGN

春秋（公元前 770～前 476 年）
青灰玉　有沁
高 6.3、宽 5.3、厚 0.8 厘米

Spring and Autumn Period (c. 770 - 476 BC)
Greyish-green jade with partial discoloration
Height, 6.3 cm; width, 5.3 cm; thickness, 0.8 cm

器作拱形，背面凹。正面饰纹较繁缛，中部以光
素宽带为界，两侧各雕兽面纹一组，兽面较为写
实。兽面左右分别雕尖喙圆目鸟首纹各一。上下
两端各有一方形凸起，凸起处中部有圆穿，穿两
侧饰"S"形纹。背面光素。此器与 1986 年江苏
吴县严山窖藏出土的双系拱形起脊饰形制相近，
当非中原之物。原器主应为吴、楚之地的高等级
贵族。此类器依形制应流行于春秋晚期。

参见：
1. 吴县文物管理委员会《江苏吴县春秋吴国玉器窖藏》,《文
物》, 1988 年第 11 期。
2. 杨建芳《论春秋晚期吴式玉器》, 见《中国古玉研究论文集》上
册——杨建芳师生古玉研究会古玉论著系列之一, 双系拱形起
脊饰, 图四三 A、图四三 B、第 240 页。台湾众志美术出版社,
2001 年。
3. 中国玉器全集编辑委员会《中国玉器全集》(3) 春秋·战国,
图版 100、第 63 页, 文、第 236 页。河北美术出版社, 1993 年。

龙纹拱形饰
ARC-SHAPED ORNAMENT WITH DRAGON DESIGN

春秋（公元前 770～前 476 年）
白玉　半透明
高 3.4、宽 4.0、璧厚 0.4 厘米

Spring and Autumn Period (c. 770 - 476 BC)
Translucent white jade
Height, 3.4 cm; width, 4.0 cm; thickness, 0.4 cm

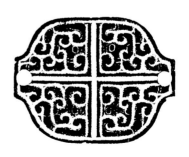

器作扁平拱形，背面凹。中部以内凹纵横"十"字
形宽栏界为四区，区内饰变形龙纹。周边以凹阴线
为缘。两端有长方形系，系内有单面钻孔。背面光
素。类似的拱形饰曾发现于江苏吴县严山窖藏、山
西太原金胜村赵卿墓、湖北随县曾侯乙墓中。

参见：
1. 吴县文物管理委员会《江苏吴县春秋吴国玉器窖藏》,《文
物》, 1988 年第 11 期。
2. 中国玉器全集编辑委员会《中国玉器全集》(3) 春秋·战国,
图版 41、第 25 页, 文、第 215 页。河北美术出版社, 1993 年。
3. 中国玉器全集编辑委员会《中国玉器全集》(3) 春秋·战国,
图版 180、第 117 页, 文、第 264 页。河北美术出版社, 1993 年。

系璧
SUSPENSION *BI*-DISK

春秋（公元前 770～前 476 年）
青玉 半透明 局部有沁
高 4.8、宽 6.6、外径 4.2、内径 1.1 厘米

Spring and Autumn Period (c. 770 - 476 BC)
Translucent green jade with partial discoloration
Height, 4.8 cm; width, 6.6 cm; diameter, 4.2 cm;
perforation diameter 1.1 cm

双面施纹。上端为出廓平顶椭圆瓶状系，系中有
双面钻圆孔。两侧为简化凤尾形出廓饰。璧双面
满饰凸起谷纹。此系璧当为楚式器，其时代应为
春秋晚期至战国早期。

圆雕猪
PIG FIGURE

春秋（公元前770～前476年）
青白玉　半透明
高1.6、长3.7厘米

Spring and Autumn Period (c. 770 - 476 BC)
Translucent pale green jade
Height, 1.6 cm; length, 3.7 cm

圆睛大耳，拱鼻阔嘴，盘尾，屈肢而卧。腹侧饰
减地云纹，背部贯天地圆孔。当为春秋晚期遗物。
此器做法与1964年山西长治分水岭84号墓所出
两件玉兽相近。

参见：
中国玉器全集编辑委员会《中国玉器全集》(3) 春秋·战国，图
版149、150，第94、95页，文、第252页。河北美术出版社，
1993年。

凤鸟纹玛瑙环
CHALCEDONY *HUAN*-RING WITH PHOENIX
DESIGN

春秋（公元前 770～前 476 年）
玛瑙 半透明
外径 7.3、内径 4.6、厚 0.6 厘米

Spring and Autumn Period (c. 770 - 476 BC)
Translucent chalcedony
Diameter, 7.3 cm; perforation diameter, 4.6 cm;
thickness, 0.6 cm

双面纹饰同。环面中部鼓起，两侧斜收。环面共
施八组相同纹饰，每组纹饰外侧为两只回首相视
的鸟首纹，内侧为勾连变形云纹。每组纹饰以亚
腰形及三角形斜格网纹为界。时代为春秋晚期。

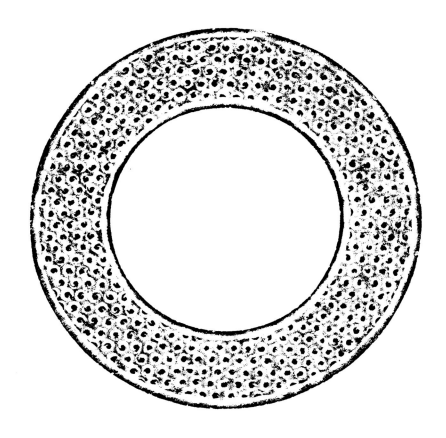

谷纹环
HUAN-RING WITH ROWS OF BUMPS

战国（公元前475～前221年）
青玉 半透明 局部有沁
外径10.4、内径6.1、厚0.4厘米

Warring States Period (c. 475 - 221 BC)
Translucent green jade with partial discoloration
Diameter, 10.4 cm; perforation diameter, 6.1 cm;
thickness, 0.4 cm

双面施谷纹，纹饰饱满，内外缘均以单阴线为界。
一侧边缘刻文"二百十九"四字。当为战国中晚
期之物。

参见：
1.傅忠谟《古玉精英》，玉环，插图四三、第80页。中华书局
（香港），1989年。
2.杨建芳《战国早期玉器》——中国古玉断代研究之五，见《中
国古玉研究论文集》下册——杨建芳师生古玉研究会古玉论著系
列之一，玉环，图六：5，第87页。台湾众志美术出版社，2001年。

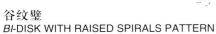

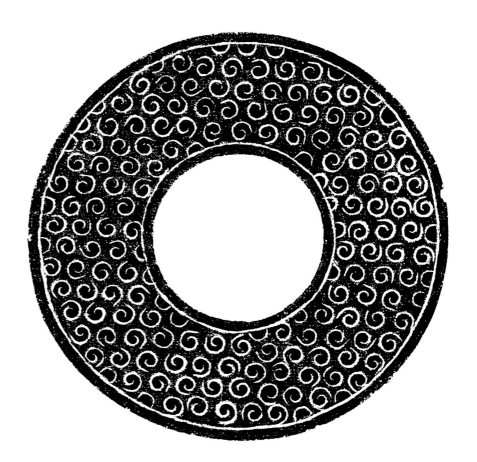

谷纹璧
BI-DISK WITH RAISED SPIRALS PATTERN

战国（公元前475～前221年）
青玉 有沁
外径11.2、内径4.5、厚0.5厘米

Warring States Period (c. 475 - 221 BC)
Green jade with partial discoloration
Diameter, 11.2 cm; perforation diameter, 4.5 cm;
thickness, 0.5 cm

双面饰谷纹，内外边缘均以单阴线为界。一侧外
缘刻"千四百九十止"六字。此璧系著名学者商
承祚先生1941年于长沙南郊购得，先生曾考证
云："所见璧上纪数之大无逾于此，此为制造或用
时行次之最末璧，故曰止，为仅见。"

参见：
1.此璧系著名学者商承祚先生之后人赠之。
2.此璧旧有著录。见商承祚《长沙古物闻见续纪》，第260页。
中华书局，1996年。
3.傅忠谟《古玉精英》，谷纹璧，插图三七、第76页。中华书
局（香港），1989年。
4.中国玉器全集编辑委员会《中国玉器全集》(3) 春秋·战国，玉璧，
图版二六一、第167页，文、第294页。河北美术出版社，1993年。

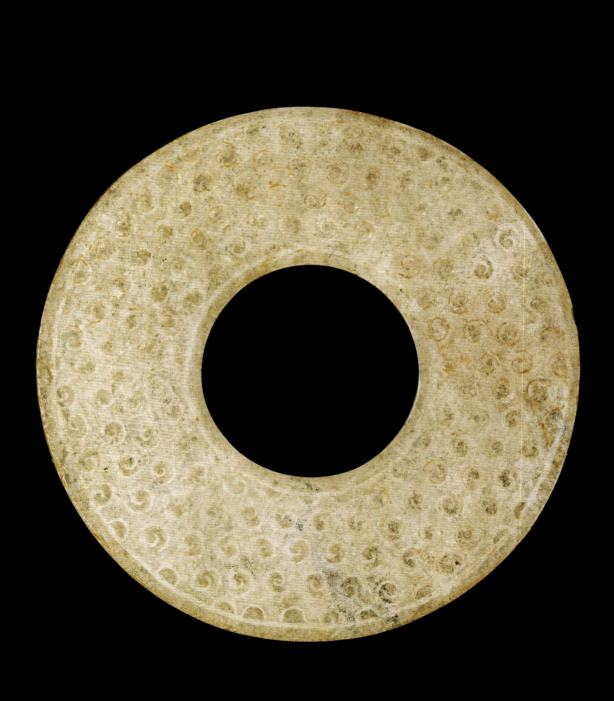

谷纹璧
BI-DISK WITH RAISED SPIRALS PATTERN

战国（公元前 475～前 221 年）
青玉　半透明　局部有沁
外径 10.9、内径 4.6、厚 0.6 厘米

Warring States Period (c. 475 - 221 BC)
Translucent green jade with partial discoloration
Diameter, 10.9 cm; perforation diameter, 4.6 cm;
thickness, 0.6 cm

双面施谷纹，纹饰饱满。制作精美，玉质温润有
泽。为战国中晚期之物。

镂空人龙合纹璧
OPENWORK *BI*-DISK WITH HUMAN AND DRAGON
DESIGN

战国（公元前 475～前 221 年）
青白玉 半透明 有沁
外径 11.1、内径 3.8、厚 0.4 厘米

Warring States Period (c. 475 - 221 BC)
Translucent pale green jade with partial discoloration
Diameter, 11.1 cm; perforation diameter, 3.8 cm;
thickness, 0.4 cm

镂空透雕，双面施纹。上下各有一立人，头梳尖
角状双髻，宽额，圆脸，直鼻，小嘴，身着圆领
窄袖长袍，腰腹间着蔽膝。立人与 1976 年河北平
山县中山国 3 号墓所出玉人接近。立人两侧镂雕
龙纹。全器质润工精，为战国中期偏晚之物。

参见：
中国玉器全集编辑委员会《中国玉器全集》(3) 春秋·战国，玉
人，图版二二九、第 149 页，文、第 282 页。河北美术出版社，
1993 年。

曲体龙形佩
PENDANT OF CURVED DRAGON

战国（公元前475～前221年）
青白玉 半透明 局部有沁
高5.5、长13.1、厚0.6厘米

Warring States Period (c. 475 - 221 BC)
Translucent pale green jade with partial discoloration
Height, 5.5 cm; length, 13.1 cm; thickness, 0.6 cm

回首，拱背，卷尾，身饰凸起谷纹。属战国晚期
器物。

参见：
1.傅熹年《古玉掇英》，镂雕虬龙形玉佩，插图五十、第111页。
中华书局（香港），1995年。
2.杨建芳《楚式玉龙佩》（下）——楚式玉雕系列之一，见《中
国古玉研究论文集》——杨建芳师生古玉研究会古玉论著系列
之一，玉龙形佩，图八十八、第40页。台湾众志美术出版社，
2001年。

绚索纹龙形佩
DRAGON PENDANT WITH SCULPTURED HEAD
AND FLUTED BODY

战国（公元前 475～前 221 年）
青白玉　半透明　局部有沁
高 11.1、首厚 1.1 厘米

Warring States Period (c. 475 - 221 BC)
Translucent pale green jade with partial discoloration
Height, 11.1 cm; head-thickness, 1.1 cm

盘体，呈圆环状。大口，有须，尖齿，鼻上扬后
卷。龙首叠于卷尾处，体作绚索状，宽扁尾，尾尖
回卷，尾饰勾连云纹。颈下有一圆穿，神态威猛。
当为战国中晚期楚国高等级贵族之物。

参见：
1. 邓淑萍《蓝田山房藏玉百选》龙首扭丝纹环，图 76、第 239
页，文、第 238 页。台湾财团法人年喜文教基金会，1995 年。
2. Alfred Salmony，Chinese Jade Through the Wei Dynarty， The Ronald
Press Company，New York，1963，Pl.24：4。
3. 杨建芳《楚式玉龙佩》（下）——楚式玉雕系列之一，见《中
国古玉研究论文集》下册——杨建芳师生古玉研究会古玉论著
系列之一，图一〇〇、第 44 页。台湾众志美术出版社，2001 年。

镂空双龙首璜
OPENWORK *HUANG*-SEGMENT WITH DRAGON-
HEAD-SHAPED ENDS

战国（公元前 475～前 221 年）
青玉　半透明
长 13.6、宽 3.8、厚 0.5 厘米

Warring States Period (c. 475 - 221 BC)
Translucent green jade
Length, 13.6 cm; width, 3.8 cm; thickness, 0.5 cm

双面纹饰同，玉质细润有光泽。两端为龙首，龙
目圆睁，张口露齿，龙身饰细线勾连云纹。身下
侧镂雕卷云纹。此器纹样及造型与安徽长丰县杨
公 2 号墓所出相似，为战国晚期所流行。

参见：
中国玉器全集编辑委员会《中国玉器全集》(3) 春秋·战国，玉
璜，彩版二九一、二九二，第 185 页，文、第 304 页。河北美
术出版社，1993 年。

双尾龙形佩
OPENWORK PENDANT OF TWO-TAILED DRAGON

战国（公元前 475～前 221 年）
青白玉 半透明
高 7.2、宽 2.8、厚 0.4 厘米

Warring States Period (c. 475 - 221 BC)
Translucent pale green jade
Height, 7.2 cm; width, 2.8 cm; thickness, 0.4 cm

镂空透雕，双面纹饰同。体作"S"形，双尾。椭
圆目，尖齿外露，角上扬回卷，屈爪，有翼。龙
角处有单钻圆孔。龙之斧式下腭为典型的楚式风
格。此器与比利时皇家历史博物馆收藏的一件龙
凤佩一侧之龙形相近。与现藏美国弗利尔美术馆
的一件镂雕虎头觿在处理手法上也多有相似之处。

参见：
1.Philippe d,Arschot,Jades Archaiques de Chine Aun Musses Royaun D,
artet D,Histoire, Brunelle, 1976, Pl.20,Cat. No.93.
2.杨建芳《楚式玉龙佩》(下)——楚式玉雕系列之一，见《中
国古玉研究论文集》下册——杨建芳师生古玉研究会古玉论著
系列之一，图一四五、第57页。台湾众志美术出版社，2001年。
3.傅熹年《古玉掇英》，插图四十三、第107页。中华书局(香
港)，1995年。

龙凤螭合雕佩
PENDANT WITH DRAGON, PHOENIX AND FELINE DESIGN

战国（公元前 475～前 221 年）
白玉 半透明
高 4.6、宽 8.6、厚 0.4 厘米

Warring States Period (c. 475 - 221 BC)
Translucent white jade
Height, 4.6 cm; width, 8.6 cm; thickness, 0.4 cm

镂空透雕，双面施纹。下部为一单首双身螭，螭首向上，双身分别向上向内卷曲。上部为两条回首相背之龙。左右两侧分别有一只竖身之凤。此器与据传出自安徽寿县、现藏美国赛克勒美术馆的一件同类器极其相似，当同为战国中期楚国贵族用物。

参见：
1. 黄浚《古玉图录初集》卷二，图三〇。
2. Thomas Lawton et al Asian Art in the ArthurM.Sackler, Washington,D.C.,1987,P.105,NO.61.
3. 杨建芳《楚式玉龙佩》（下）——楚式玉雕系列之一，见《中国古玉研究论文集》下册——杨建芳师生古玉研究会古玉论著系列之一，图一六一、第62页。台湾众志美术出版社，2001年。

双首龙形佩
OPENWORK PENDANT OF TWO-HEADED
DRAGON

战国（公元前475～前221年）
青白玉　半透明
高3.1、宽4.5、厚0.4厘米

Warring States Period (c. 475 - 221 BC)
Translucent pale green jade
Height, 3.1 cm; width, 4.5 cm; thickness, 0.4 cm

镂空透雕，双面饰纹。双首相对，曲体连身。尖
牙利齿，龙之下腭呈斧头形，为典型的楚式风格。
身饰变形勾连云纹，爪下饰斜格网纹。时代为战
国中期。

松石镂空双身龙形佩
OPENWORK DRAGON WITH ONE HEAD AND TWO
BODIES

战国（公元前475～前221年）
松石
高 4.0、宽 4.9、厚 0.3 厘米

Warring States Period (c. 475 - 221 BC)
Turquoise
Height, 4.0 cm; width, 4.9 cm; thickness, 0.3 cm

镂空透雕，双面纹饰同。单首双身，龙首位于中
部，龙身向左右分开，身尾连为一体，左右有对
称尖足。本器制作精美，与美国赛克勒美术馆收
藏的一件玉质双身龙佩极为相似，当为战国晚期
楚国贵族用物。

参见：
1.Max Loehr,Ancient Chinese Jades,Fogg Art Muse um,Harvard University,
1975,PP.286 & 290,NO.423.
2.杨建芳《楚式玉龙佩》（下）——楚式玉雕系列之一，见《中
国古玉研究论文集》——杨建芳师生古玉研究会古玉论著系列
之一，图一〇二、第45页。台湾众志美术出版社，2001年。

松石团身螭虎佩
FELINE TIGER PENDANT WITH TUCKED BODY

战国（公元前475～前221年）
松石
宽4.0、厚0.3厘米

Warring States Period (c. 475 - 221 BC)
Turquoise
Width, 4.0 cm; thickness, 0.3 cm

团身回首衔尾状。双目凸睛，小耳上耸，头顶以
阴线刻出长角，背部有阴刻脊线，两旁有双弧线。
体后部外侧有镂雕花朵，花朵正背面均刻阴线
纹。此器造型、纹饰俱佳，为难得的松石精品。依
其形制、纹样应为楚式，流行于战国晚期。

凤形佩
PHOENIX-SHAPED PENDANT

战国（公元前 475～前 221 年）
青白玉 半透明 局部有沁
长 13.6、厚 0.4 厘米

Warring States Period (c. 475 - 221 BC)
Translucent pale green jade with partial discoloration
Length, 13.6 cm; thickness, 0.4 cm

体作"S"形，凤首回转前视，钩喙，颈有飘羽，
卷尾倒翻。凤身一面饰勾鳞纹，另一面饰细密阴
线纹。凤身中部有一系孔。整器质地温润，制作
极精。依其形制、纹样及工艺，当为楚式器，时
代为战国中晚期。

凤纹蝶形佩
BUTTERFLY-SHAPED PENDANT WITH PHOENIX DESIGN

战国（公元前475～前221年）
青白玉 半透明 局部有黑沁
高 2.0、长 5.0、宽 4.0 厘米

Warring States Period (c. 475 - 221 BC)
Translucent pale green jade with partial black markings
Height, 2.0 cm; length, 5.0 cm; width, 4.0 cm

蝶面上部高浮雕一曲体卧伏的凤鸟，蝶身饰排列整齐的浅浮雕双联谷纹。依其形式及纹样，当为楚式器。蝶中孔径小于2厘米，显系仅作装饰之用，故称之为蝶形佩。

勾连谷纹管形饰
TUBE-SHAPED PENDANT WITH INTERLOCKING RAISED SPIRALS

战国（公元前475～前221年）
白玉 半透明
高 4.1、上径 2.2、下径 2.7 厘米

Warring States Period (c. 475 - 221 BC)
Translucent white jade
Height, 4.1 cm; diameter, 2.2 cm (top), 2.7 cm (bottom)

上下端有宽沿，器表遍饰浮雕的四联谷纹，但上端首行饰横置双联谷纹。器中有上下贯穿圆孔。勾联谷纹最早见于楚式玉雕中，双联者常见，三联者少见，而四联谷纹则罕见。此件应为楚式器。

羽觞杯
CUP WITH WING-SHAPED HANDLE

战国（公元前475～前221年）
水晶 透明
高2.5、径6.6、宽8.8厘米

Warring States Period (c. 475 - 221 BC)
Transparent crystal
Height, 2.5 cm; diameter, 6.6 cm; width (with handle),
8.8 cm

圆形杯身，宽耳，圈形浅底内凹。双耳面各透雕
四个大尾谷纹，以阴刻变形云纹相连。杯内底部
以圆形双阴线为界，内饰卷云纹。杯外壁上部饰
宽带状浅浮雕云纹，中部饰勾连谷纹，近底处饰
索纹。整器饰纹繁缛、华丽。依其所饰当为楚人
之物。水晶制品如此精美者极少见。

圆雕蝉
CICADA FIGURE

西汉（公元前206～公元8年）
青白玉 半透明 有沁
高4.5、宽2.3、厚1.2厘米

Western Han (206 BC - AD 8)
Translucent pale green jade with partial discoloration
Height, 4.5 cm; width, 2.3 cm; thickness, 1.2 cm

圆睛凸起，敛翼，露背，并以极细线条刻画翼脉。
腹部针嘴、三对蝉足、软腹腹节俱全。首尾间贯
穿天地孔。形象写实，与徐州狮子山楚王陵所出
白玉蝉极相似。

参见：
1.狮子山楚王陵考古发掘队《徐州狮子山西汉楚王陵发掘》，
蝉，彩色插页二：3(W1：95)，文、第17页。《文物》，1998年第
8期。台湾《中国文物世界》第185期。
2.傅忠谟《古玉精英》，蝉，图72、第153页。中华书局（香
港），1989年。

圆雕立人
STANDING HUMAN FIGURE

西汉（公元前 206～公元 8 年）
青白玉
高 4.3 厘米

Western Han (206 BC - AD 8)
Translucent pale green jade
Height, 4.3 cm

高挽双髻，面目清秀，有须。身着左衽长衫，腰
间束带，拢袖而立。汉代圆雕玉人发掘出土者较
少，此应为汉代早中期之物。

羽人骑辟邪
PLUMED RIDER ON *BIXIE*-CHIMERA

西汉（公元前206～公元8年）
青白玉 半透明
高5.7、长8.9厘米

Western Han (206 BC - AD 8)
Translucent pale green jade
Height, 5.7 cm; length, 8.9 cm

表面多处有受沁形成的灰白斑。辟邪呈匍匐行走状，昂首，额凸起，双睛圆睁，张口露齿，吐舌，舌尖上翘，长须下垂，双耳后耸，胸肌发达。背上骑一羽人，头发后飘，肩和腰部生羽翅。全器造型凶悍、逼真，是罕见的汉玉佳作。

圆雕虎
TIGER FIGURE

西汉（公元前206～公元8年）
青玉
高3.0、长5.3厘米

Western Han (206 BC - AD 8)
Green jade
Height, 3.0 cm; length, 5.3 cm

昂首匍匐，双耳微竖，口大张，露出锋利的牙齿。背部雕出脊线，全身毛发的雕刻方式与陕西兴平霍去病墓前的石虎以及咸阳市博物馆收藏的汉代虎纹空心有相似之处。

参见：
王仁波《秦汉文化》162页，图四：148～149，图二、三。上海学林出版社、上海科技教育出版社，2001年。

松石辟邪
TURQUOISE *BIXIE*-CHIMERA

西汉（公元前 206～公元 8 年）
松石
高 3.8、长 13.2 厘米

Western Han (206 BC - AD 8)
Turquoise
Height, 3.8 cm; length, 13.2 cm

侧首前伸，独角，双目炯炯，张口露齿卷舌。肩生双翼，尾部分叉倒卷。一足前伸，三足微屈，作奔走状。此为十分罕见的汉代松石圆雕珍品。

圆雕双角瑞兽
MYTHICAL ANIMAL FIGURE WITH TWO HORNS

西汉（公元前 206～公元 8 年）
青玉
高 3.1、长 5.8 厘米

Western Han (206 BC - AD 8)
Green jade
Height, 3.1 cm; length, 5.8 cm

双目前视，口微张，双角后伏，屈肢伏卧。迄今
面世的汉代圆雕瑞兽类玉作少之又少，此可谓难
得一见之物。

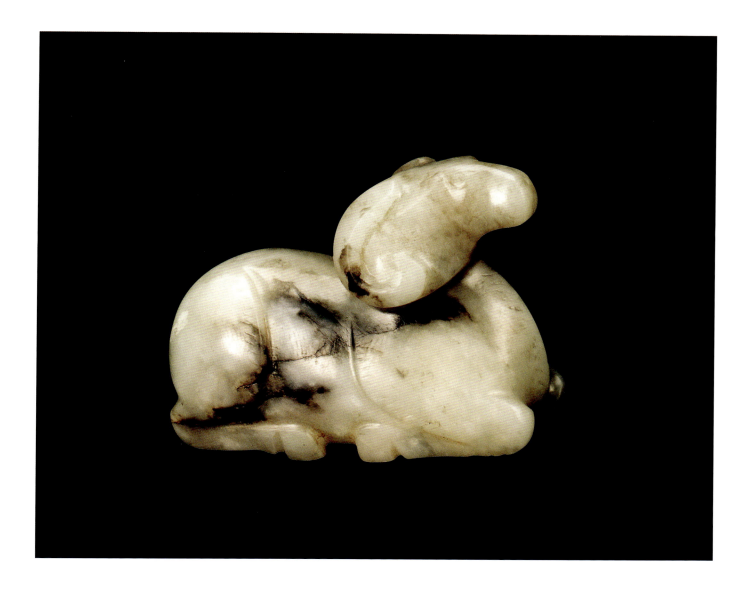

圆雕卧羊
CROUCHING RAM

西汉（公元前 206～公元 8 年)
青玉
高 3.9、长 5.6 厘米
Western Han (206 BC - AD 8)
Green jade
Height, 3.9 cm; length, 5.6 cm

昂首挺胸，屈肢跪卧。长颈，弯角回盘，肥臀短
尾。形象生动。

长角卧羊
CROUCHING RAM WITH LONG HORNS

西汉（公元前 206～公元 8 年）
青白玉 半透明 局部有沁
高 4.8、长 10.8 厘米

Western Han (206 BC - AD 8)
Translucent pale green jade with partial discoloration
Height, 4.8 cm; length, 10.8 cm

圆雕。侧首前视，小耳，长角后伏。四肢内屈跪
卧，体态肥硕，为汉代圆雕佳作。

圆雕奔羊
RUNNING RAM

西汉（公元前206～公元8年）
青白玉
高6.3、长11.0、宽4.0厘米

Western Han (206 BC - AD 8)
Pale green jade
Height, 6.3 cm; length, 11.0 cm; width, 4.0 cm

体态肥硕，昂首前探，小耳，短颈，短尾伏于臀间，四肢屈伸有度作奔走状，极显健美之态。

圆雕象
ELEPHANT FIGURE

西汉（公元前 206～公元 8 年）
青白玉 局部有沁
高 6.1、长 8.4 厘米

Western Han (206 BC - AD 8)
Pale green jade with partial discoloration
Height, 6.1 cm; length, 8.4 cm

细目大耳，长鼻后卷。短柱足，腹下垂。神情安
详，憨态可掬。整器造型极其写实，一反汉初玉
作多凶悍、威猛之态，实为难得。

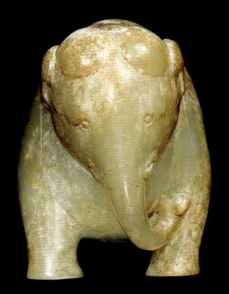

圆雕鸟
BIRD FIGURE

西汉（公元前 206～公元 8 年)
青白玉 半透明
高 4.5、长 9.0、宽 6.5 厘米

Western Han (206 BC - AD 8)
Translucent pale green jade
Height, 4.5 cm; length, 9.0 cm; width, 6.5 cm

短喙披冠，敛翼宽尾，屈爪于腹下。羽间与尾上
有层层叠压的宽条状羽束，胸腹部、翅前端、尾
端阴刻密集细线。刻画细腻传神。

参见：
1. 中国玉器全集编辑委员会《中国玉器全集》(4) 秦·汉——
南北朝，图版 150，第 111 页，文，第 275 页。河北美术出版社，
1993 年。
2. 邓淑萍《蓝田山房藏玉百选》，图 39、90，第 264～269 页。
台湾财团法人年喜文教基金会，1995 年。
3.《中国肖生玉雕》，图版 53，第 86、87 页。香港艺术馆，1996 年。

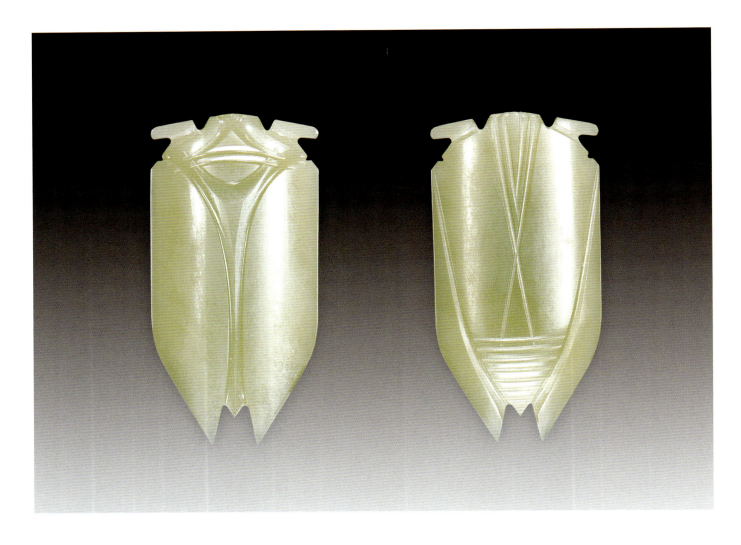

青玉蝉
CICADA-SHAPED PENDANT

西汉（公元前206～公元8年）
青玉 半透明
长6.4、宽3.3、厚1.0厘米

Western Han (206 BC - AD 8)
Translucent green jade
Height, 6.4 cm; width, 3.3 cm; thickness, 1.0 cm

以减地阴线刻画蝉首、针状口、翅、腹节等，扁
平条状双目制作精细。为西汉晚期至东汉初较常
见之物。

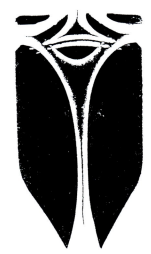

系璧
SUSPENSION *BI*-DISK

西汉（公元前206～公元8年）
青白玉　半透明　有沁
高6.8、外径6.2、内径2.0、厚0.4厘米

Western Han (206 BC - AD 8)
Translucent pale green jade with partial discoloration
Height, 6.8 cm; diameter, 6.2 cm; perforation diameter,
2.0 cm; thickness, 0.4 cm

双面施勾连谷纹，上端廓外有一桃形坠系。璧作
为礼器的功能至西汉时已消失，代之成为富贵人
家的赏玩装饰之物。

镂空透雕龙凤纹璧
BI-DISK WITH OPENWORK DRAGON AND
PHOENIX

西汉（公元前 206～公元 8 年）
青玉
外径 10.4、内径 4.5、厚 0.5 厘米

Western Han (206 BC - AD 8)
Green jade
Diameter, 10.4 cm; perforation diameter, 4.5 cm;
thickness, 0.5 cm

镂空透雕，双面饰纹。三条虬龙与三只凤鸟的身
体相互盘绕，其间又有丝绦穿梭其中。整器构图
巧妙，富有想象力。此种构图及雕刻手法见于西
汉初，如广州南越王墓东侧室的"右夫人"B 组
组玉佩中的两件透雕环，即是采用此种手法处
理的。

参见：
广州西汉南越王墓博物馆、香港中文大学文物馆《南越王墓玉
器》，图版 138～140，文、第 269～270 页。两木出版社，1991 年。

兽面纹出廓璧
BI-DISK WITH OPENWORK ANIMAL MASK ABOVE

西汉（公元前 206～公元 8 年）
青灰玉 通体有沁
高 7.8、璧外径 4.2、厚 0.8 厘米

Western Han (206 BC - AD 8)
Greyish-green jade with alteration on entire surface
Height, 7.8 cm; diameter, 4.2 cm; thickness, 0.8 cm

双面纹饰同。上部圭形，兽首纹，局部透雕。下
部为谷纹璧。此件当为作嵌镶用的小型铺首。

双龙首扭丝纹璜
FLUTED *HUANG*-SEGMENT WITH DRAGON-HEAD-
SHAPED ENDS

西汉（公元前206～公元8年）
青白玉 半透明 局部有沁
高5.8、径0.9厘米

Western Han (206 BC - AD 8)
Translucent pale green jade with partial discoloration
Height, 5.8 cm; diameter, 0.9 cm

两端为龙首，身饰扭丝纹。扭丝纹亦称绞丝纹，此
种手法始见于东周，汉时较为流行。

女羽人
KNEELING PLUMED FEMALE FIGURE

东汉（公元 25～220 年）
青白玉
高 9.0、宽 2.5 厘米

Eastern Han (AD 25 - 200)
Pale green jade
Height, 9.0 cm; shoulder width, 2.5 cm

玉质晶莹，局部有灰白沁色。踞坐，头戴冠，直鼻小口。身着长衣，两肩生翼，双手作捧物状。通体抛磨光洁，处理手法细腻。

圆雕猪
PIG FIGURE

东汉（公元 25～220 年）
青白玉　半透明
高 2.5、长 11.0、宽 2.5 厘米

Eastern Han (AD 25 - 200)
Translucent pale green jade
Height, 2.5 cm; length, 11.0 cm; width, 2.5 cm

条状，卧姿，造型简洁，为东汉时期常见之物。

参见：
1.《中国肖生玉雕》，图版 36，第 68、69 页。香港艺术馆，1996 年。
2. 西安市文物保护考古所《西安文物精华玉器》，第 114 页。世界图书出版西安公司，2004 年。
3. 中国玉器全集编辑委员会《中国玉器全集》(4) 秦·汉—南北朝，图版 245、第 176 页，文、第 306 页。河北美术出版社，1993 年。

伏兔
CROUCHING HARE

东汉（公元 25～220 年）
青白玉 有褐斑
高 2.5、长 4.5、宽 2.5 厘米

Eastern Han (AD 25 - 200)
Pale green jade with brown suffusion
Height, 2.5 cm; length, 4.5 cm; width, 2.5 cm

圆雕。凹睛伏耳，曲肢短尾，作俯卧状。腹下部
有一横钻圆孔。

参见：
《中国肖生玉雕》，图版 39，第 70、71 页。香港艺术馆，1996 年。

镂空龙虎纹璧
BI-DISK WITH OPENWORK DRAGON AND TIGER

东汉（公元25～220年）
青白玉 半透明 局部有沁
外径11.0、内径2.1、厚0.5厘米

Eastern Han (AD 25 - 200)
Translucent pale green jade with partial discoloration
Diameter, 11.0 cm; perforation diameter, 2.1 cm;
thickness, 0.5 cm

廓内透雕一龙一虎。虎披飘鬃，肩生羽翼；龙披
锦鳞，须角俱全。龙行雨，虎生风，神态飘逸，动
感十足。璧三面出廓，更添神韵。

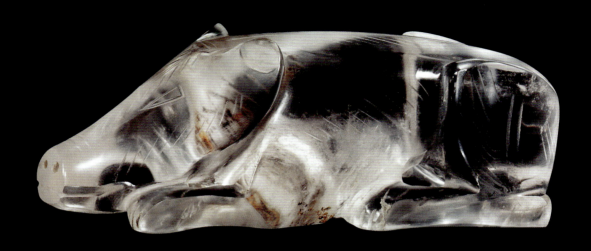

水晶猪
CRYSTAL PIG FIGURE

东汉（公元25～220年）
白水晶 透明
高 2.7、长 7.7、宽 2.5 厘米

Eastern Han (AD 25 - 200)
Transparent crystal
Height, 2.7 cm; length, 7.7 cm; width, 2.5 cm

长鼻前伸。凹鼻孔，扁口，三角眼，双耳上竖。四
肢屈伏，短尾。

水晶耳杯
CRYSTAL CUP WITH HANDLE

东汉（公元 25～220 年）
白水晶 透明
高 3.4、长 10.2、宽 8.2 厘米

Eastern Han (AD 25 - 200)
Transparent crystal
Height, 3.4 cm; length, 10.2 cm; width, 8.2 cm

椭圆杯身，宽直耳，浅平底。两侧耳近杯沿处各
有三个三角形镂孔，耳面饰对称三角形几何纹，
底部饰一周三角形几何纹。

圆雕辟邪
BIXIE-CHIMERA IN THE ROUND

两晋南北朝（公元 265～589 年）
青褐玉 有沁
高 3.2、长 6.0、宽 2.8 厘米

Six Dynasties (AD 265 - 589)
Brownish-green jade with partial discoloration
Height, 3.2 cm; length, 6.0 cm; chest-width, 2.8 cm

作卧伏状。头部有角，翅翼后展，盘尾屈爪。此
件器形与北京故宫博物院藏青玉异兽相类似，为
两晋南北朝时极少见的珍品。

龟纽印
SEAL WITH TURTLE-SHAPED HANDLE

两晋南北朝（公元 265～589 年）
青褐玉
高 3.0、印面宽 2.6～2.7 厘米

Six Dynasties (AD 265 - 589)
Brownish-green jade
Height, 3.0 cm; seal-length, 2.7 cm; seal-width, 2.6 cm

龟形纽，印身作正方形，无字。此印与江苏南京
郭家山东晋墓所出极为接近。器表整体呈墨色，
似经过特殊处理。

参见：
《中国美术全集》工艺美术编·9·玉器，图版201、第111页，
文、第72页。文物出版社，1986年。

方形胡人击拍板带銙
SQUARE BELT PLAQUE WITH FOREIGN MUSICIAN PLAYING *PAIBAN*-DRUM

唐（公元618～907年）
青白玉　半透明
高5.0、宽5.2、厚0.6厘米

Tang (AD 618 - 907)
Translucent pale green jade
Height, 5.0 cm; width, 5.2 cm; thickness, 0.6 cm

方形，浮雕。胡人高鼻深目，络腮胡须，长卷发以绦带束之，束发丝带于前额正中处有一圆形饰物。身着华丽胡服，足蹬高靴，盘腿坐于一长方织毯上。拍板竖置于左肩处，右手击之。此带銙与1987年西安市西郊丈八沟唐代窖藏中发现的伎乐白玉带銙相似。但质地、纹样、做工更优。

参见：
1.刘云辉《北周隋唐京畿玉器》——杨建芳师生古玉研究会古玉图录系列之一，图版T72、73，第55页。重庆出版社，2000年6月。
2.傅熹年《古玉掇英》，唐代雕胡人乐舞玉带，插图八十八、第201页。中华书局（香港），1995年。

半圆形胡人吹笙带铸
SEMI-CIRCULAR BELT PLAQUE WITH FOREIGN
MUSICIAN PLAYING *SHENG*-REED PIPE

唐（公元 618～907 年）
青白玉
高 2.5、宽 3.4、厚 0.7 厘米

Tang (AD 618 - 907)
Pale green jade
Height, 2.5 cm; width, 3.4 cm; thickness, 0.7 cm

半圆形，正面边缘以减地阴线为界。胡人长卷发，
三角目，高鼻。身着紧身胡服，肩披飘带，足蹬
小尖靴，交足盘膝而坐。双手持笙，作吹奏状。此
类带铸曾出于西安市西郊唐墓中，为盛唐时流行
式样。

参见：
刘云辉《北周隋唐京畿玉器》——杨建芳师生古玉研究会古玉
图录系列之一，图版T107、第71页。重庆出版社，2000年。

半圆形胡人弹琵琶带铸
SEMI-CIRCULAR BELT PLAQUE WITH FOREIGN
MUSICIAN PLAYING *PIPA*-STRING INSTRUMENT

唐（公元 618～907 年）
青白玉
高 2.5、宽 3.4、厚 0.7 厘米

Tang (AD 618 - 907)
Pale green jade
Height, 2.5 cm; width, 3.4 cm; thickness, 0.7 cm

半圆形，正面边缘以减地阴线为界。胡人卷发披
肩，身着紧身胡服，足蹬长筒靴。左腿屈膝，右
腿内屈平置，坐于椭圆形茵毯之上，怀抱琵琶弹
奏。背面四角有牛鼻钻孔。

参见：
1. 刘云辉《北周隋唐京畿玉器》——杨建芳师生古玉研究会古
玉图录系列之一，图版T105、第70页。重庆出版社，2000年。
2. 中国玉器全集编辑委员会《中国玉器全集》(5) 隋·唐—明，
图版53、第33页，图版63、第38页。河北美术出版社，1994
年（香港版）。

白玉花卉纹梳背
COMB BACK WITH FLOWER DESIGN

唐（公元618～907年）
白玉 半透明
高5.1、长21.2、厚0.3厘米

Tang (AD 618 - 907)
Translucent white jade
Height, 5.1 cm; length, 21.2 cm; thickness, 0.3 cm

片状，弧背，下端有扁平的榫，以供镶嵌梳齿。双
面雕刻同样的花卉纹。

参见：
中国玉器全集编辑委员会《中国玉器全集》(5) 隋·唐—明，图
版17～19，第11、12页。河北美术出版社，1994年（香港版）。

白玉凤鸟海棠钗（1对）
PAIR OF HAIRPINS WITH PHOENIX AND
CRABAPPLE FLOWER DESIGN

唐（公元618～907年）
白玉 半透明
通长14.3、钗头长7.5、宽2.8、厚0.3厘米

Tang (AD 618 - 907)
Translucent white jade
Length, 14.3 cm (pin), 7.5 cm (pinhead); width, 2.8 cm;
thickness, 0.3 cm

钗头两面纹饰同。以阴线刻丹凤朝阳，凤下有海
棠。钗体金质。此钗与北京故宫博物院藏唐代青
玉鸟纹钗及1981年西安市唐兴庆宫遗址出土的玉
凤纹簪头风格相同，为唐代妇女饰物。

参见：
1.中国玉器全集编辑委员会《中国玉器全集》（5）隋·唐—明，
图版13、15、第8、9页，文、第231页。河北美术出版社，1994
年（香港版）。
2.西安市文物保护考古所《西安文物精华·玉器》，图版、第84
页，文、第154页。世界图书出版西安公司，2004年。

白玉凤鸟纹钗首
HAIRPIN HEAD WITH PHOENIX DESIGN

唐（公元 618～907 年）
白玉 局部有沁
长 10.6、宽 5.8、厚 0.2 厘米

Tang (AD 618 - 907)
White jade with partial discoloration
Length, 10.6 cm (pin); width, 5.8 cm; thickness, 0.2 cm

镂刻，双面纹饰同。以阴线刻丹凤朝阳。凤衔花
梗，昂首卧于花叶之上。凤首前及腹下各有一朵
牡丹，朵间有梗蔓相连。其下钗体已失。当为唐
时妇女头面饰物。

参见:
1.中国玉器全集编辑委员会《中国玉器全集》(5) 隋·唐—明，
图版 13、15，第 8、9 页，文、第 231 页。河北美术出版社，1994
年（香港版）。

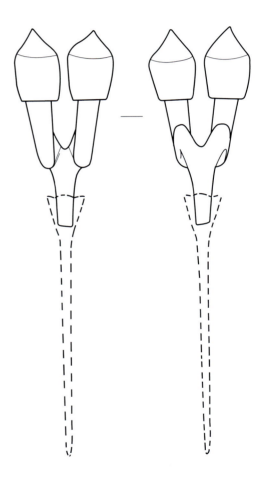

白玉双簪首
DOUBLE-HEADED HAIRPIN

唐（公元618～907年）
白玉 半透明
高5.7厘米

Tang (AD 618 - 907)
Translucent white jade
Height, 5.7 cm

双圆柱状，尖顶簪首。为唐时妇女头面饰品。

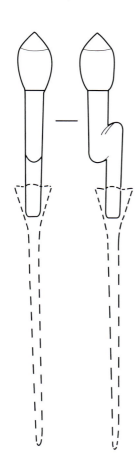

白玉单簪首
SINGLE-HEADED HAIRPIN

唐（公元618～907年）
白玉　半透明
高5.2厘米

Tang (AD 618 - 907)
Translucent white jade
Height, 5.2 cm

圆柱状尖顶簪首。为唐时妇女头面饰品。

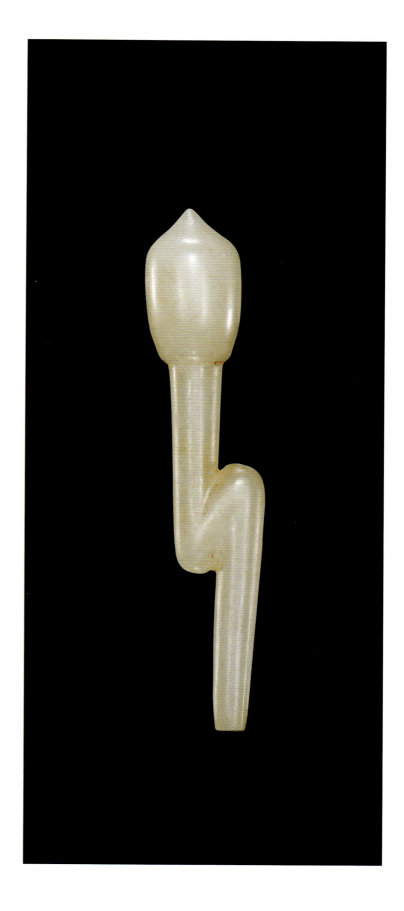

团身卧马
RECUMBENT HORSE WITH TUCKED BODY

唐（公元 618～907 年）
青褐玉 有黑斑及裂纹
高 3.0、横宽 6.5、纵宽 5.6 厘米

Tang (AD 618 - 907)
Brownish-green jade with black markings and cracks
Height, 3.0 cm; width, 6.5 cm (frontal view), 5.6 cm
(side view)

团身盘体，形态优美，细节雕刻细腻。

参见：
1.叶义《中国玉雕》，图版131，第142、143页。香港艺术馆，
1983 年。
2.《中国肖生玉雕》，图版65，第96、97页。香港艺术馆，1996
年。
3.另可参见① Watt, James, Chinese Jade from the Collection of the
Seattle Art Museum.(Seattle: Seattle Art Museum,1989),nos.32a,
32b & 32c.西雅图博物馆:盘状骆驼。② Watt, James, Chinese Jades
from Han to Ching.(New York: The Asia Society,1980),no.32.官富
藏:唐马。③ Ibid.,NO.64.

羊形坠饰
RAM-SHAPED PENDANT

唐（公元 618～907 年）
青玉 局部有沁
长 4.1、宽 1.7、厚 3.0 厘米

Tang (AD 618 - 907)
Green jade with partial discoloration
Length, 4.1 cm; width, 1.7 cm; thickness, 3.0 cm

抿口，凹圆睛，盘角。四肢内屈作卧伏状。背部
有长方形天地孔。当为小型坠饰。

弯角卧羊
CROUCHING RAM WITH BENT HORNS

唐～宋（公元 618～1279 年）
青白玉　局部有沁
高 2.8、长 4.3、宽 2.0 厘米

Tang - Song (AD 618 - 1279)
Pale green jade with partial discoloration
Height, 2.8 cm; length, 4.3 cm; width, 2.0 cm

羊首伏于胸前，长角弯于颈间，四肢回蜷而卧。体
态丰盈，刀法简练，颇具宋人之风。此件的制作
年代应略晚于《古玉掇英》所收宋代青玉卧羊。

参见：
1.《中国肖生玉雕》图版 67，第 98、99 页。香港艺术馆，1996
年。
2.傅熹年《古玉掇英》，图 121，文、第 231 页。中华书局(香港)，
1995 年。

鸟形鸠首
BIRD-SHAPED CANE FINIAL

唐～宋（公元 618～1279 年）
黄白玉　有沁
高 4.0、长 5.0、宽 3.0 厘米

Tang - Song (AD 618 - 1279)
Yellowish-white jade with partial discoloration
Height, 4.0 cm; length, 5.0 cm; width, 3.0 cm

短喙，小圆睛，敛翅翘尾，屈爪于腹下。腹下有
方形座，座中有圆管形孔。此器为鸠杖首。

参见：
《中国肖生玉雕》图版 77，第 106、107 页。香港艺术馆，1996 年。

童子形杖首
BOY SHAPED CANE FINIAL

宋（公元960～1279年）
青白玉　局部有沁
高8.2、底径2.4厘米

Song (AD 960 - 1279)
Pale green jade with partial discoloration
Height, 8.2 cm; cane diameter, 2.4 cm

小童形。齐额短披发，圆睛，凸鼻头，环形耳。身
着窄袖长衣，腰间束带。盘足坐于覆莲之上，双
手横持短笛吹奏。莲下为中空柱状，柱下端两侧
有圆穿，作穿铆固定之用。

刻铭手镯
BRACELET WITH INSCRIPTIONS

宋宣和二年（公元1120年）
灰白玉 有黑斑
高2.0、外径6.3厘米

Song, 2nd year of Xuanhe Reign (AD 1120)
Greyish-white jade with black fleckings
Height, 2.0 cm; diameter, 6.3 cm

镯体宽而扁平，器表抛光。镯面环刻"宣和贰年
之仲氏作弄玉百串"十二字。宣和，为宋徽宗年
号，宣和二年当为公元1120年。弄玉，应是玩赏
用玉之意。

回首骆驼
RECUMBENT CAMEL WITH BACK-TURNED HEAD

宋（公元 960～1279 年）
青白玉 有褐斑
高 4.0、长 6.5、宽 3.5 厘米

Song (AD 960 - 1279)
Pale green jade with brown patches
Height, 4.0 cm; length, 6.5 cm; width, 3.5 cm

团身，长颈后曲，驼首回伏于驼峰之上，四肢卧
于腹下，卷尾盘于臀侧。此器做工精致，刻画形
神俱佳。

参见：
《中国肖生玉雕》，图版87，第114、15页。香港艺术馆，1996年。

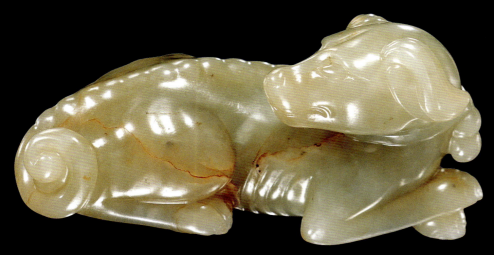

卷尾卧犬
CROUCHING DOG WITH COILED TAIL

宋（公元 960～1279 年）
青白玉　半透明
高 4.2、长 8.4 厘米

Song (AD 960 - 1279)
Translucent pale green jade
Height, 4.2 cm; length, 8.4 cm

曲颈回首，大耳后伏，前肢叠搭，后肢前屈，细
长尾盘卷于腹侧。雄性。颈间围软质项圈，坠葫
芦形响铃。整器强悍中透着柔顺，喻意吉祥，颇
显宋人写实之风。

大耳卧犬
RECLINING DOG WITH BIG EARS

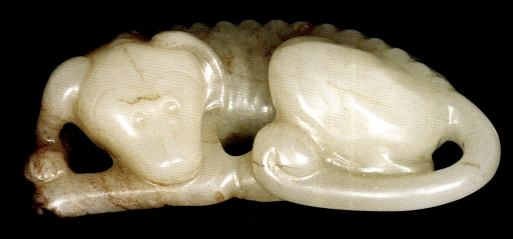

宋（公元 960～1279 年）
青白玉　半透明
高 2.0、长 6.0、宽 3.0 厘米

Song (AD 960 - 1279)
Translucent pale green jade
Height, 2.0 cm; length, 6.0 cm; width, 3.0 cm

侧首伏于前肢，大耳下垂，前肢交叠，曲身蜷体，
长尾回卷臀部。颇具宋器风格。

参见：
1.叶义《中国玉雕》，图版 135，第 146、147 页。香港艺术馆，
1983 年。
2.《中国肖生玉雕》，图版 99，第 122、123 页。香港艺术馆，1996
年。
3.《好古敏求》——敏求精舍三十五周年纪念展，图版 108。香
港艺术馆，1995 年。

三羊开泰
RAM WITH TWO LAMBS

宋（公元960～1279年）
白玉 半透明
高 5.5、长 7.5、宽 3.8 厘米

Song (AD 960 - 1279)
Translucent white jade
Height, 5.5 cm; length, 7.5 cm; width, 3.8 cm

三羊相倚而卧，母羊昂首，双角后弯，长须下垂。
两小羊一倚前胸，一倚尾后。全器优美恬静，神
形兼备。

参见：
1.《中国肖生玉雕》，图版107，第130、131页。香港艺术馆，
1996年。
2.《中国肖生玉雕》，图版90，第116、117页。香港艺术馆，1996
年。
3.①叶义《中国玉雕》，图版142，第154、155页。香港艺术
馆，1983年。麦雅理藏：宋代白玉羊。②Keverne,Roger.Han to
Song Chinese Jade by McElney In Jade.1991. ③Watt,James,Chinese
Jades From Han To Ching.(New York:The Asia Society,1980),NO.58.

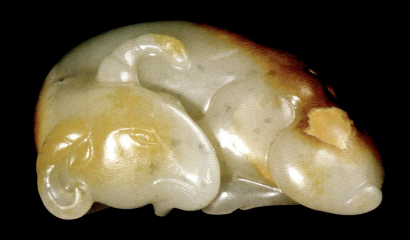

大尾卧羊
CROUCHING RAM WITH BIG TAIL

宋（公元960～1279年）
青玉 有褐斑
高 2.5、长 5.5、宽 3.5 厘米

Song (AD 960 - 1279)
Green jade with brown patches
Height, 2.5 cm; length, 5.5 cm; width, 3.5 cm

曲体盘卧，侧首低垂，颏下垂短须。角弯盘耳后，
肥尾微翘。神态安详，惹人怜爱。

参见：
1.叶义《中国玉雕》，图版139，第150、151页。香港艺术馆，
1983年。
2.《中国肖生玉雕》，图版92，第118、119页。香港艺术馆，1996年。

长角跪羊
KNEELING RAM WITH LONG HORNS

宋（公元 960～1279 年）
青白玉　局部有沁
高 4.5、长 5.5、宽 3.0 厘米

Song (AD 960 - 1279)
Pale green jade with partial discoloration
Height, 4.5 cm; length, 5.5 cm; width, 3.0 cm

昂首，凸睛，颏下有长髯，扭丝状长角微后卷，肥臀短尾。四肢回屈跪伏。背腹处有扁圆天地孔。造型乖巧温顺，雕工精致细腻。

参见：
《中国肖生玉雕》图版 91，第 116、117 页。香港艺术馆，1996 年。

回首短尾羊
RAM WITH BACK-TURNED HEAD AND SHORT TAIL

宋（公元 960～127 年）
青白玉　半透明
高 3.5、长 7.0、宽 2.8 厘米

Song (AD 960 - 1279)
Translucent pale green jade
Height, 3.5 cm; length, 7.0 cm; width, 2.8 cm

回首侧视，颏下垂须，索状盘角，四肢内屈跪卧，肥尾短翘。造型生动传神，做工精湛细腻，是典型的宋代玉作。

参见：
《中国肖生玉雕》图版 95，第 120、121 页。香港艺术馆，1996 年。

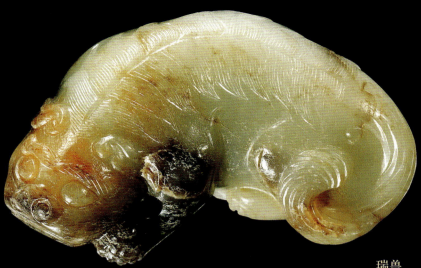

瑞兽
AUSPICIOUS ANIMAL

宋（公元960～1279年）
青玉　有褐斑
高3.0、长7.5、宽4.0厘米

Song (AD 960 - 1279)
Green jade with brown patches
Height, 3.0 cm; length, 7.5 cm; width, 4.0 cm

首伏于前肢间，阔口短耳，躬身，鬃披背上，长
尾曲盘于腹侧。颈下有穿孔。

参见：
1.《中国文物集珍》——敏求精舍银禧纪念展，图版213、第419
页。香港艺术馆，1985年。
2.《中国肖生玉雕》，图版84，第110、111页。香港艺术馆，1996
年。
3.《好古敏求》——敏求精舍四十周年纪念展。图版108，宋代
影青褐彩虎、犬，香港艺术馆，2001年。

瑞兽
AUSPICIOUS ANIMAL

宋（公元960～1279年）
青白玉　半透明
高2.2、长6.8、宽3.6厘米

Song (AD 960 - 1279)
Translucent pale green jade
Height, 2.2 cm; length, 6.8 cm; width, 3.6 cm

兽首伏于前肢，圆睛小耳，脊骨外露，长尾盘于
腹侧。颈下系金锭。腹下部有一横贯圆穿。

参见：
《中国肖生玉雕》，图版86，第112、113页。香港艺术馆，1996年。

卧犬
CROUCHING DOG

宋（公元 960～1279 年）
青黄玉 有褐红斑
高 2.0、长 6.8、宽 3.8 厘米

Song (AD 960 - 1279)
Yellowish-green jade with brownish-red patches
Height, 2.0 cm; length, 6.8 cm; width, 3.8 cm

前肢屈而交叠，侧首回伏于前肢之上。长耳，凹
圆睛，长尾翻卷于身侧。犬身俏色，更显得生动
活泼。

参见：
《中国肖生玉雕》图版107、第130、131页。香港艺术馆，1996年。

交吻鸳鸯
KISSING MANDARIN DUCKS

宋（公元 960～1279 年）
青白玉 半透明 有红褐斑
高 2.6、长 5.2、宽 4.0 厘米

Song (AD 960 - 1279)
Translucent pale green jade with reddish-brown
markings
Height, 2.6 cm; length, 5.2 cm; width, 4.0 cm

雌雄鸳鸯，侧首交吻。羽翼刻画细致，造型别致。

参见：
《中国肖生玉雕》，图版120，第140、141页。香港艺术馆，1996年。

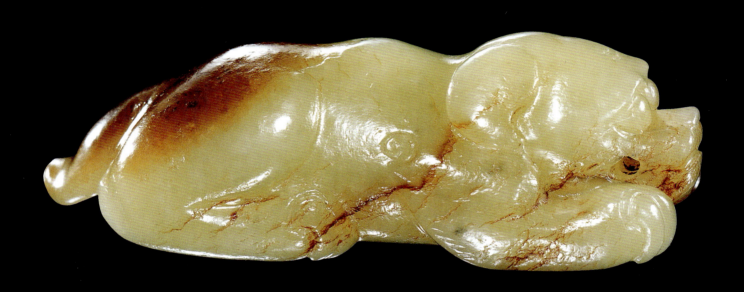

瑞兽
AUSPICIOUS ANIMAL

宋（公元 960～1279 年)
黄玉 有褐斑
高 2.8、长 7.5、宽 3.3 厘米

Song (AD 960 - 1279)
Yellow jade with brown patches
Height, 2.8 cm; length, 7.5 cm; width, 3.3 cm

卧姿，首伏于前肢间。凸睛前视，叶状小耳、扁
阔短尾。嘴下有一圆穿。造型细腻，刻画遒劲。

参见：
1.《中国肖生玉雕》，图版 106，第 130、131 页。香港艺术馆，
1996 年。
2. Morgan, Brian, Naturalism and Archaism, (1995), NO. 48.

鳜鱼
MANDARIN FISH

宋（公元 960～1279 年）
青白玉 半透明 有褐斑
高 3.0、长 5.3、宽 1.8 厘米

Song (AD 960 - 1279)
Translucent pale green jade with brown markings
Height, 3.0 cm; length, 5.3 cm; width, 1.8 cm

圆雕。体态肥硕，张口翘尾，腹身以交错阴线饰鳞
片，背腹鳍棘俱全。器身中部有一长方形天地孔。

参见：
《中国肖生玉雕》，图版 121，第 142、143 页。香港艺术馆，1996 年。

青皮大虾
FRESH-WATER SHRIMP

宋（公元960～1279年）
青玉 半透明
长8.1厘米

Song (AD 960 - 1279)
Translucent green jade
Length, 8.1 cm

躬腰探首，活灵活现。处理手法极为写实。

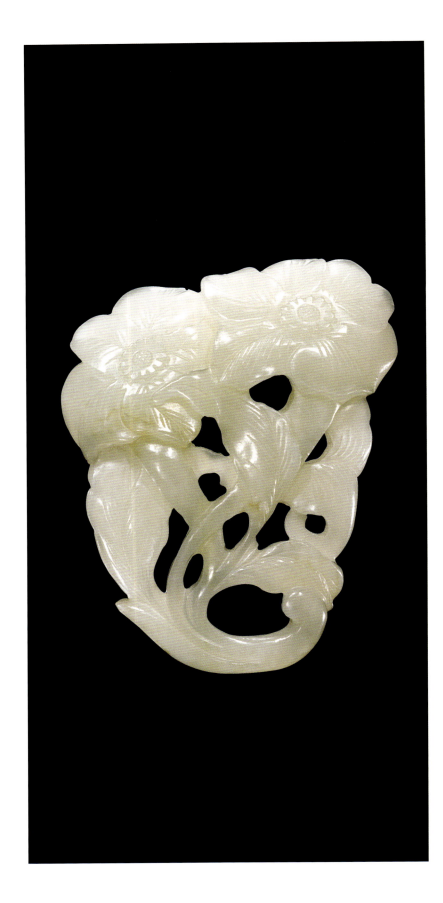

镂空缠枝凌霄花
ORNAMENT WITH OPENWORK TENDRIL AND
FLOWER DESIGN

宋（公元 960～1279 年）
青白玉 半透明
高 6.0、宽 4.5、厚 0.4 厘米

Song (AD 960 - 1279)
Translucent pale green jade
Length, 6.0 cm; width, 4.5 cm; thickness 0.4 cm

通体镂雕两枝阔叶有蔓凌霄花。阴线示花叶，琢磨精细。背部内凹。此类玉佩为宋、辽、金时所习见。

鱼桃坠饰
PENDANT SET OF FISH AND PEACH

辽（公元 916～1125 年）
青白玉 半透明
鱼长 6.0、宽 2.6、厚 0.7 厘米
桃长 2.0、宽 3.5、厚 1.0 厘米

Liao (AD 916 - 1125)
Translucent pale green jade
Fish: Length, 6.0 cm; width, 2.6 cm; thickness 0.7 cm
Peach: Length, 2.0 cm; width, 3.5 cm; thickness 1.0 cm

上系为阔身宽尾之鱼，鱼口衔回卷的水草。下坠
为双桃，桃中有圆形贯孔。为辽金时习见的成组
坠饰。

水晶熊
GILDED CRYSTAL BEAR

辽（公元916~1125年）
白水晶 透明
高4.8、长7.8、宽4.0厘米

Liao (AD 916 - 1125)
Transparent crystal
Height, 4.8 cm; length, 7.8 cm; width, 4.0 cm

圆睛凸目，小耳，颈有披鬃。前肢蹲，后肢卧伏。
全身多处尚存鎏金痕迹。此件熊面部特征与1978
年内蒙古巴林右旗白音汉窖藏所出白玉兽（应为
熊）极似。辽时的水晶饰品存世不多，此器体硕
工精，体表鎏金，更可谓少见之物。

参见：
1.中国玉器全集编辑委员会《中国玉器全集》(5)隋·唐—明，
图版143、第92页，文、第270页。河北美术出版社，1994年
（香港版）。

雌雄双雁
PAIRED WILD GEESE

辽金（公元 916～1234 年）
白玉　半透明
高 4.0、宽 3.3、厚 1.0 厘米

Liao-Jin (AD 916 - 1234)
Translucent white jade
Height, 4.0 cm; width, 3.3 cm; thickness 1.0 cm

圆睛长喙，敛翅，作卧姿。雌雄相偎，口衔水草，
神态安详。水草上部有一圆穿，下部有斜穿孔。做
工精巧，刻画细致，为辽金时期的玉作精品。

鸳鸯踏荷带銙
BELT PLAQUE WITH MANDARIN DUCKS ON LOTUS LEAF

辽金（公元916～1234年）
青白玉 半透明
带銙铜扣：高4.1、宽4.5、厚1.4厘米
带銙：高3.7、宽4.2、厚0.9厘米

Liao-Jin (AD 916 - 1234)
Translucent pale green jade
Copper rim: height, 4.1 cm; width, 4.5 cm; thickness, 1.4 cm;
Jade plaque: Height, 3.7 cm; width, 4.2 cm; thickness, 0.9 cm

雌雄鸳鸯踏荷而立。颈披锦羽，双翅乍扬，交喙互吻，亲密无间。形象逼真传神，刻画写实细腻。镶于方形铜扣之内，背面有条状横穿。

鸳鸯踏荷带銙
BELT PLAQUE WITH MANDARIN DUCKS ON LOTUS LEAF

辽金（公元916～1234年）
玛瑙 半透明
带銙铜扣：高4.1、宽4.5、厚1.4厘米
带銙：高3.8、宽4.2、厚1.1厘米

Liao-Jin (AD 916 - 1234)
Translucent chalcedony
Copper rim: height, 4.1 cm; width, 4.5 cm; thickness, 1.4 cm;
Jade plaque: Height, 3.8 cm; width, 4.2 cm; thickness, 1.1 cm

与上件形制相同，当属同一副玉带。

荷花孔雀嵌饰
OPENWORK PENDANT WITH PEACOCK AND LOTUS

金（公元1115～1234年）
青白玉 半透明
高9.5、宽4.2、厚2.3厘米

Jin (AD 1115 - 1234)
Translucent pale green jade
Height, 9.5 cm; width, 4.2 cm; thickness, 2.3 cm

镂雕，椭圆条状。下端一孔雀立于山石之上，回首，翘翅，长尾。孔雀身侧及上端有三朵盛开的荷花及叶蔓。雀翅及尾部刻画极精，全器多以管钻深挖镂雕法制作。为少见的金代玉件佳作。

持叶童子
BOY HOLDING LOTUS

元（公元 1271～1368 年）
青白玉 局部有沁
高 6.1、厚 2.1 厘米

Yuan (AD 1279 - 1368)
Pale green jade with partial discoloration
Height, 6.1 cm; thickness, 2.1 cm

五官面相颇存宋代遗风，隆鼻，元宝状口，下颏
宽硕。但脑门上以小块凸起示发髻，手掌与袖口
同宽却是典型元人玉作的表现手法。小童上着开
襟长袖紧身短衣，下穿肥裤，裤下露足，着靴。颈
下围角巾状饰物，饰物系结于后背，结下有长条
形双飘带垂至腿部。左手下垂，掌中有鱼。右手
持一长梗有脉蔓草，上举附于脑后。

龙形炉顶
DRAGON-SHAPED INCENSE BURNER LID

元（公元 1271～1368 年）
白玉 半透明
高 3.5、长 4.2、宽 2.2 厘米

Yuan (AD 1271 - 1368)
Translucent white jade
Height, 3.5 cm; length, 4.2 cm; width, 2.2 cm

采用多层立体镂雕法制作。龙行在上，腾于云朵
之间，昂首张口，双角，颈有飘鬣，曲身探爪，尾
回卷收于首下。底椭圆形内凹，一端有二对横向
牛鼻穿孔，一端为一对竖向牛鼻穿孔，以供镶系。
整器浑厚、奔放，为典型的元人玉作。北京故宫
博物院藏有一件青玉镂空龙凤纽，应为炉顶。上
海博物馆也藏有一件青白玉龙纹炉顶。此三件龙
形炉顶均为元代玉器佳作。

参见：
1. 中国玉器全集编辑委员会《中国玉器全集》(5) 隋·唐—明，
图版 167、第 110 页，文、第 278 页。河北美术出版社，1994 年
(香港版)。
2. 王正书《"炉顶"、"帽顶"辨识》，见上海博物馆《中国隋唐
至清代玉器学术研讨会论文集》，图一一、第 282 页。上海古籍
出版社，2002 年。

凤形炉顶
PHOENIX-SHAPED INCENSE BURNER LID

元（公元 1271～1368 年）
白玉 半透明
高 4.4、长 4.0、宽 2.0 厘米

Yuan (AD 1271 - 1368)
Translucent white jade
Height, 4.4 cm; length, 4.0 cm; width, 2.0 cm

多层立体镂雕。凤鸣于花朵枝叶之上，凤首披飘
羽，颈围锦毛。凤首下有五瓣花卉一朵，凤身两
侧饰荷叶、莲篷。底作荷叶形内凹，两端各有一
对横向牛鼻穿孔。整体和谐，粗放中不失优美。

祥云麒麟
QILIN (KYLIN)-UNICORN ON CLOUD

元（公元 1271～1368 年）
青白玉
高 4.5、长 5.6、宽 1.2 厘米

Yuan (AD 1271 - 1368)
Pale green jade
Height, 4.5 cm; length, 5.6 cm; width, 1.2 cm

麒麟是传说中的瑞兽。阔口露齿，隆眉，额上生
权角，颈后飘鬣，挺胸昂首，足踏祥云，威严中
透着祥瑞。

子母瑞兽
AUSPICIOUS ANIMAL WITH YOUNG

元（公元 1271～1368 年）
青白玉　半透明
高 2.8、长 6.0、宽 5.0 厘米

Yuan (AD 1271 - 1368)
Translucent pale green jade
Height, 2.8 cm; length, 6.0 cm; width, 5.0 cm

母子相偎，作蹲伏状。如意鼻头，脊骨外露，均
属较早之特征。而圆睁双睛与逗点耳朵的手法则
流行于宋元之时。

参见：
《中国肖生玉雕》，图版 117，第 138、139 页。香港艺术馆，1996 年。

踞坐瑞兽
KNEELING AUSPICIOUS ANIMAL

元（公元 1271～1368 年）
白玉　半透明　有沁
高 4.2、长 5.0、宽 2.0 厘米

Yuan (AD 1271 - 1368)
Translucent white jade with partial discoloration
Height, 4.2 cm; length, 5.0 cm; width, 2.0 cm

整器以子玉雕成，保留了卵石的原始状态。鼻孔、
口侧、耳涡的处理保留了较早时期的遗风，卷云
纹尾梢回附于腹侧。背腹间有天地孔。

卧兽
CROUCHING AUSPICIOUS ANIMAL

元（公元 1271～1368 年）
青白玉　半透明
高 3.0、长 4.5、宽 3.0 厘米

Yuan (AD 1271 - 1368)
Translucent pale green jade
Height, 3.0 cm; length, 4.5 cm; width, 3.0 cm

独角，脑后披球状鬣毛，圆睁双目，耳朵卷曲，如
意形宽鼻头，扁平阔口。屈肢侧卧，左后肢作搔
痒状，卷云形分叉尾回贴至腹前部。前肢处有系
孔。面部开相及分叉卷云形尾的处理手法，是典
型的元代风格。

鳜鱼
MANDARIN FISH

元（公元 1271～1368 年）
青玉 有灰褐斑
高 4.0、长 6.5、宽 1.3 厘米

Yuan (AD 1271 - 1368)
Green jade with greyish-brown patches
Height, 4.0 cm; length, 6.5 cm; width, 1.3 cm

厚唇阔口，曲尾上翘，背腹鳍棘俱全，腹身以斜
方格阴线饰鳞片。器身中部有天地孔。

参见：
《中国肖生玉雕》，图版122，第142、143页。香港艺术馆，1996年。

俏色龙首螭纹带钩
BELT HOOK WITH DRAGON-SHAPED HEAD AND
FELINE DESIGN

元（公元 1271～1368 年）
青白玉 半透明
长 13.0、宽 3.5、厚 3.6 厘米

Yuan (AD 1271 - 1368)
Translucent pale green jade
Length, 13.0 cm; width, 3.5 cm; thickness, 3.6 cm

琵琶形，龙首为钩，阔嘴宽鼻，双叉形角。钩身
曲伏一俏色螭龙。背有长方形纽。依形制当为元
代之物，亦称"教子"龙钩。

参见：
1.中国玉器全集编辑委员会《中国玉器全集》(5) 隋·唐—明，
图版169、第111页，文、第278页。河北美术出版社，1994年
（香港版）。

狮纹牌饰
SQUARE PLAQUE WITH OPENWORK LION
DESIGN

元（公元 1271～1368 年）
青玉 半透明
高 4.0、宽 3.0、厚 0.48 厘米

Yuan (AD 1271 - 1368)
Translucent pale green jade
Height, 4.0 cm; width, 3.0 cm; thickness, 0.48 cm

透雕方牌。牌中为一立狮，狮首稍侧，前肢上举，
后肢屈伏。狮身两侧有柞叶，叶面延至边框。牌
面凸起。依其形制，当为元末之物。

白玉童子
BOY FIGURE

明（公元 1368～1644 年）
白玉 半透明 局部有黃斑
高 6.2、寬 3.5、厚 2.3 厘米

Ming (AD 1368 - 1644)
Translucent white jade with yellow streaks
Height, 6.2 cm; width, 3.5 cm; thickness, 2.3 cm

童子頭冠軟翅幞頭，面露笑容。身着窄袖長衣，外
罩半袖襦衫。雙手持折技長蔓仙草。

连生贵子
BOY WITH LOTUS

明（公元 1368～1644 年）
淡青黄玉 半透明
高 4.5、宽 4.0 厘米

Ming (AD 1368 - 1644)
Translucent light greenish - yellow jade
Height, 4.5 cm; width, 4.0 cm

垂髫小童，盘腿坐于莲叶之上。宽袖长衫，面露
笑容。右手持莲梗，莲叶向上卷伏于童背。红莲
托小童，逗人喜爱，寓意连生贵子。莲叶下有蚌
（谐音胖），又称莲生胖娃。为民间祈子而作。

参见：
1. 叶义《中国玉雕》，图版 167，香港艺术馆，1983 年。
2. Watt, James, Chinese Jades From Han To Ching. (New York: The Asia
Society, 1980), NO.96.

马上封侯
MONKEY ON HORSE

明（公元 1368～1644 年）
青灰玉 有黑斑
高 6.3、长 8.5、底宽 3.0 厘米

Ming (AD 1368 - 1644)
Greyish-green jade with black markings
Height, 6.3 cm; length, 8.5 cm; bottom-width, 3.0 cm

马卧伏，曲颈垂首，竖耳披鬃，马尾回卷于马臀
一侧。马背上伏卧一只侧首短尾小猴。小猴右前
肢抓握马鬃，意谓"马上封侯"。此类造型明代开
始流行。

参见：
Watt, James, Chinese Jades From Han To Ching. (New York, The Asia
Society, 1980), NO. 70.

白玉双狮
LION WITH CUB

明（公元 1368～1644 年）
白玉 半透明
高 4.5、长 7.5 厘米

Ming (AD 1368 - 1644)
Translucent white jade
Height, 4.5 cm; length, 7.5 cm

双狮回首相向。大狮口衔花草，小狮卧于臀侧。刻
画细腻写实。亦称"太狮少狮"。

参见：
1.《中国文物集珍》——敏求精舍银禧纪念展览，图版216，第
423、424 页。
2.《历代文物萃珍》——敏求精舍三十周年纪念展，图版217，
第452、453 页。

瑞兽
AUSPICIOUS ANIMAL

明（公元 1368～1644 年）
青白玉 半透明
高 2.8、长 5.0、宽 4.0 厘米

Ming (AD 1368 - 1644)
Translucent pale green jade
Height, 2.8 cm; length, 5.0 cm; bottom-width, 4.0 cm

侧首盘体。独角，扁平阔嘴，脊骨隆起，硕尾回卷。
前肢间有一穿孔。刻画细致。

参见：
《中国肖生玉雕》，图版141，第158、159页。香港艺术馆，1996年。

马上封侯
MONKEY ON HORSE

明（公元 1368～1644 年)
青白玉 半透明 有褐斑
高 4.5、长 6.5、宽 2.5 厘米

Ming (AD 1368 - 1644)
Translucent pale green jade with brown markings
Height, 4.5 cm; length, 6.5 cm; width, 2.5 cm

马屈肢回首，猴蹲踞于马臀，造型生动别致。"马
上封侯"的艺术造型流行于明清两代，寓吉祥、即
刻高升之意。

参见：
《中国肖生玉雕》，图版152，第166、167页。香港艺术馆，1990年。

童子牧牛
BUFFALO BOY

明（公元 1368～1644 年)
青白玉 半透明 有褐斑
高 4.2、长 9.5、宽 5.5 厘米

Ming (AD 1368 - 1644)
Translucent pale green jade with brown patches
Height, 4.2 cm; length, 9.5 cm; width, 5.5 cm

水牛卷尾团身，作休憩状。童子身负斗笠，手持
横笛，卧于牛背之上。表现出悠闲恬淡的意境。

参见：
1.《历代文物萃珍》——敏求精舍三十周年纪念展，图版219，
第454、455页。香港艺术馆，1990年。
2.《中国肖生玉雕》，图版154，第166、167页。香港艺术馆，
1996年。

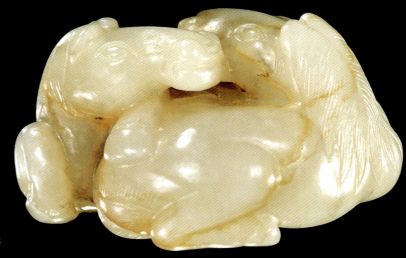

回首双卧马
TWO INTERTWINING CROUCHING HORSES

明（公元 1364~1644 年）
青白玉　半透明
高 3.0、长 4.5、宽 4.0 厘米

Ming (AD 1368 - 1644)
Translucent pale green jade
Height, 3.0 cm; length, 4.5 cm; width, 4.0 cm

两马回首相依盘卧，一马前蹄搭于另一马马臀之
上，怡然而自得。双马盘结，为自宋以降坊间常
见的题材。

参见：
《中国肖生玉雕》，图版 136，第 154、155 页。香港艺术馆，1996 年。

太狮少狮
LION WITH CUB

明（公元 1368～1644 年）
青玉 半透明
高 6.2、长 7.0、宽 3.5 厘米

Ming (AD 1368 - 1644)
Translucent pale green jade
Height, 6.2 cm; length, 7.0 cm; width, 3.5 cm

太狮蹲坐，前肢直立。宽眉深目，张口露齿，扁
平鼻，脑后披三络长鬣，四肢处饰火焰纹。少狮
立于太狮尾上。太狮脊骨突出是仿唐宋手法，而
足底平整、扁平鼻及火焰纹等又为典型的明代
风格。

翘首卧鹿
CROUCHING DEER WITH RAISED HEAD

明（公元 1368～1644 年）
白玉 半透明
高 6.3、长 8.0 厘米

Ming (AD 1368 - 1644)
Translucent white jade
Height, 6.3 cm; length, 8.0 cm

跪卧，翘首，垂耳，作聆听状。质佳工精，为明
玉上品。

参见：
《中国文物集珍》——敏求精舍银禧纪念展览，图版215、第421页。

独角瑞兽
UNICORN

明（公元 1368～1644 年）
白玉 半透明
高 3.0、长 5.0、宽 2.3 厘米

Ming (AD 1368 - 1644)
Translucent white jade
Height, 3.0 cm; length, 5.0 cm; width, 2.3 cm

伏卧状。羊首，圆晴小耳，口衔灵芝，颏下有须。
独角后俯于背脊，足、蹄俱全，短尾垂于臀部。

参见：
《中国肖生玉雕》，图版168，第176、177页。香港艺术馆，1996年。

黄玉鸟
BIRD FIGURE

明（公元 1368～1644 年）
黄玉 半透明
高 3.5、长 7.5、宽 3.0 厘米

Ming (AD 1368 - 1644)
Translucent yellow jade
Height, 3.5 cm; length, 7.5 cm; width, 3.0 cm

短喙，大眼前视，敛翅，宽翘尾，屈爪于腹下。整
器圆润如脂，流畅自然。

参见：
《中国肖生玉雕》，图版161，第172、173页。香港艺术馆，1996年。

交吻双鸟
TWO KISSING BIRDS

明（公元 1368～1644 年）
青白玉 半透明
高 5.6、宽 2.8、厚 1.2 厘米

Ming (AD 1368 - 1644)
Translucent pale green jade
Height, 5.6 cm; width, 2.8 cm; thickness, 1.2 cm

一雌一雄，左右相依，双喙交吻。整器勾勒匀称，
静谧中透着祥和、满足，人性化的处理手法可谓
独具匠心。

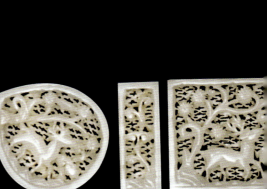

白玉透雕松鹿纹玉带
BELT SET OF SIXTEEN PIECES WITH OPENWORK DEER DESIGN

明（公元 1368～1644 年）
白玉 半透明
每件厚 0.65～0.7 厘米（详见附表）

Ming (AD 1368 - 1644)
Translucent white jade
Thickness, 0.65 - 0.7 cm

此副玉带现存十六铸。除两件辅弼（窄长条形铸）外，均以双层透雕松鹿纹为主题纹饰，以山石、梅花、竹子、蕉叶等为辅助纹饰。构图和谐，层次丰富，纹饰、图案栩栩如生，立体感强。长方形铸八件，主题纹饰多为双鹿，以山石相隔，一鹿前视，一鹿回顾。桃形铸四件（失两件），主题纹饰均为单鹿，姿态各不相同。铊尾2件，主题纹饰为雌雄双鹿，一前一后，回首相顾作奔跑状。窄长条形铸两件（失两件），均雕山石蕉叶纹。

明人张自烈《正字通》戌集铸字条下云"明制，革带前合处曰三台，左右排三圆桃，排方左右曰鱼尾，有辅弼二小方，后七枚，前大小十三枚。"依制，可知明代玉带整副为二十铸，由长方形铸八件（一曰三台，后排七铸曰排方），桃形铸六件（曰圆桃），铊尾两件（曰鱼尾），窄长条形铸四件（曰辅弼）组成。依明制，知此副玉带失桃形铸二、窄长条形铸二。

此副玉带与1975年江西省南昌蛟桥公社出土的一副保存完好的白玉透雕松鹿纹玉带（二十铸），在玉质、纹饰、构图、雕工方面相当接近，当同为明代中期藩王所佩白玉带的典型代表。

参见：
彭适凡、陈建平《江西明宁藩王墓出土的两副玉带》，见上海博物馆《中国隋唐至清代玉器学术研讨会论文集》，第71～77页。上海古籍出版社，2002年。

白玉透雕松鹿纹玉带尺寸表
（厘米）

编号	长	宽	备注
1	9.0	4.6	三台
2	4.5	1.7	辅弼
3	5.0	4.5	圆桃
4	5.0	4.4	圆桃
5	9.6	4.7	鱼尾（铊尾）
6	7.3	4.6	排方
7	7.6	4.6	排方
8	7.5	4.6	排方
9	7.9	4.6	排方
10	6.6	4.6	排方
11	7.2	4.6	排方
12	7.6	4.6	排方
13	9.7	4.6	鱼尾（铊尾）
14	5.1	4.4	圆桃
15	4.9	4.3	圆桃
16	4.6	1.7	辅弼

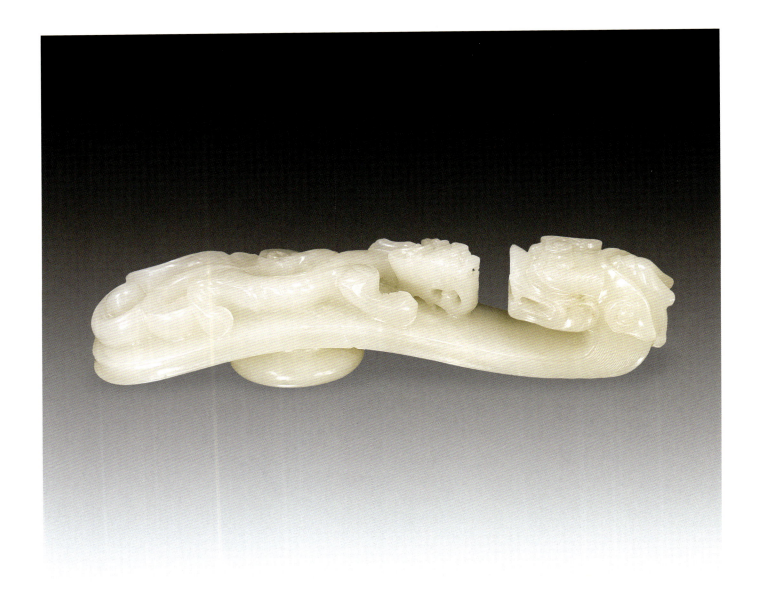

白玉龙首螭纹带钩
BELT HOOK WITH DRAGON-SHAPED HEAD AND
FELINE DESIGN

明（公元 1368～1644 年）
白玉 半透明
高 2.6、长 12.7 厘米

Ming (AD 1368 - 1644)
Translucent white jade
Height, 2.6 cm; length, 12.7 cm

钩首做龙首形，回首与钩身所饰的俯卧螭相望。
钩身前窄后宽，下附圆形纽，纽身宽大。依形制
当为元末明初之物。亦称"教子"龙钩。

参见：
王正书、周丽娟《宋元明清玉雕带钩的断代》——明代带钩，见
上海博物馆，《中国隋唐至清代玉器学术研讨会论文集》，2002年。

倚坐老翁
OLD MAN LEANING ON SMALL TABLE

清（公元 1644～1911 年）
青玉
高 6.4、宽 7.5 厘米

Qing (AD 1644 - 1911)
Green jade
Height, 6.4 cm; width, 7.5 cm

长髯老翁，怡然而坐，左手抚膝，右臂倚案。面
相为康熙朝所习见。

参见：
1. 叶义《中国玉雕》，图版176、第192页。香港艺术馆，1983年。
2.《玲珑玉雕》，图版34、第53页。香港大学美术博物馆，1996年。

张仙送子
SON-OFFERING DEITY ZHANG XIAN

清（公元 1644~1911 年）
白玉 半透明
高 6.0 厘米

Qing (AD 1644 - 1911)
Translucent white jade
Height, 6.0 cm

张仙头佩软巾，慈眉善目，长髯。身着宽袖长衫，
腰结丝绦。右臂上举，手托弹丸，左手执弓。小童
侧首仰视，一手托竹篓，一手执花结。全器质如凝
脂，白玉无瑕，做工精细，为康乾朝玉作精品。

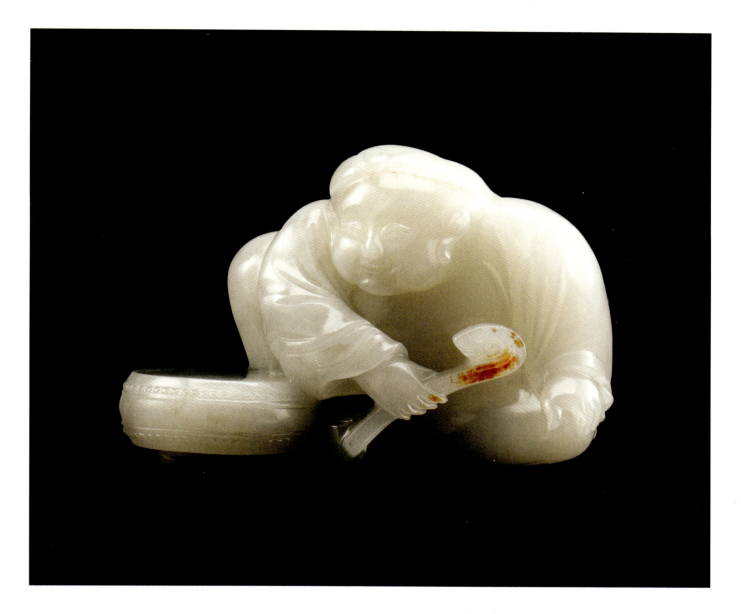

童子戏鼓
BOY PLAYING WITH DRUM

清（公元 1644～1911 年)
白玉　半透明
高 4.3、宽 7.0 厘米

Qing (AD 1644 - 1911)
Translucent white jade
Height, 4.3 cm; width, 7.0 cm

小童宽眉细目，隆鼻小口，颊露酒涡，喜笑颜开。
额系胡式毛状飘带饰物，结于脑后。身着宽袖长
衫，腰间束带。左手抚膝，右手执云纹如意，身旁
平置羯鼓。造型优美，刻画传神，当做于明末清初。

参见:
1.叶义《中国玉雕》，图版175、第192页。香港艺术馆，1996年。
2.《玲珑玉雕》，图版27、第51页。香港大学美术博物馆，1996年。

麻姑献寿
IMMORTAL MAGU CELEBRATING LONGEVITY

清（公元 1644～1911 年）
白玉 有褐斑
高 5.6、宽 3.0、厚 2.0 厘米

Qing (AD 1644 - 1911)
White jade with brown flecks
Height, 5.6 cm; width, 3.0 cm; thickness, 2.0 cm

身姿秀丽。右手提花篮，左手执长蔓灵芝。身边
与足下饰祥云，身后倚一梅花鹿。刻画传神，做
工细腻，为康乾时期珍品佳作。

参见：
《玲珑玉雕》，图版 39、第 63 页。香港大学美术博物馆，1996 年。

莲台坐佛
SEATED BUDDHA ON LOTUS THRONE

清（公元 1644～1911 年）
青白玉
高 11.5、宽 7.0 厘米

Qing (AD 1644 - 1911)
Pale green jade
Height, 11.5 cm; width, 7.0 cm

头戴如意宝冠，琥珀帽纽。身着宽衣，肩披帛带，
胸前饰璎珞，双腕佩镯，双手叠置腹间，赤足，结
跏趺坐于莲台，宝相庄严。此乃佛堂陈设。

参见：
1.《清朝瑰宝》，图版 241、第 377 页。香港艺术馆，1992 年。
2.《玲珑玉雕》，图版 35、第 59 页。香港大学美术博物馆，1996 年。

童子击鼓
BOY STRIKING DRUM

清（公元 1644～1911 年）
白玉 半透明
高 3.6、宽 6.0 厘米

Qing (AD 1644 - 1911)
Translucent white jade
Height, 3.6 cm; width, 6.0 cm

童子头梳双髻，宽额，蒜头鼻，满面笑容。身着
束腰上衣，下穿肥裤，倚鼓蹲踞。左足置于鼓前，
右足屈于身后，右手执短棒于鼓前，左手持如意
于鼓后。鼓顶悬磬，磬下垂彩结流苏。寓意"吉
庆如意"。鼓下有镂雕鼓座。鼓座后侧卧一长耳卷
尾小犬。此器童子面部开相颇似上海博物馆藏清
代执芭蕉童子。

参见：
1.《玲珑玉雕》，图版 37、第 61 页。香港大学美术博物馆，1996 年。
2. 朱淑仪《上海博物馆藏玉童研究》，图三二、第 205 页，文，
第 194 页。见上海博物馆《中国隋唐至清代玉器学术研讨会论
文集》，上海古籍出版社，2002 年。

老翁负妻
OLD MAN CARRYING WIFE ON BACK

清（公元 1644～1911 年）
白玉
高 6.8、宽 2.9 厘米

Qing (AD 1644 - 1911)
White jade
Height, 6.8 cm; width, 2.9 cm

老翁长髯飘飘，负妻于背上，二人侧首凝眸，戏
谑人生。亦称"老背少"。

参见：
《玲珑玉雕》，图版42、第66页。香港大学美术博物馆，1996年。

俏色蟾蜍
THREE-FOOTED TOAD

清（公元 1644～1911 年）
白玉 有褐斑
高 2.0、长 4.5、宽 3.0 厘米

Qing (AD 1644 - 1911)
White jade with brown flecks
Height, 2.0 cm; length, 4.5 cm; width, 3.0 cm

三足蟾蜍，爪持俏色石榴，寓意"丁财两旺"。质
如凝脂，为清代苏州坊间代表作。

参见：
1.叶义《中国玉雕》，图版284、第296页。香港艺术馆，1983
年。
2.《中国肖生玉雕》，图版178，第186、187页。香港艺术馆，
1996年。

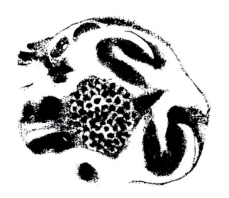
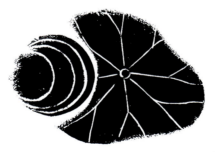

白玉蟾蜍
TOAD

清（公元 1644~1911 年）
白玉 半透明
高 2.1、长 5.0 厘米

Qing (AD 1644 - 1911)
Translucent white jade
Height, 2.1 cm: length, 5.0 cm

蟾蜍卧于莲叶之上，右前爪伏于蚌上，屈肢欲跃。
寓"连生胖娃"之意。

参见：
叶义《中国玉雕》，图版 289，香港艺术馆，1983 年。

戏水鸳鸯
MANDARIN DUCK WITH LOTUS

清（公元 1644～1911 年）
白玉 半透明 有褐斑
高 3.0、长 4.5、宽 2.0 厘米

Qing (AD 1644 - 1911)
Translucent white jade with brown flecks
Height, 3.0 cm; length, 4.5 cm; thickness, 2.0 cm

鸳鸯卧伏，体侧伴有莲花。颈与莲花间有穿孔。质佳工精，为清代苏州坊间代表作。

参见：
《中国肖生玉雕》，图版181，第188、189页。香港艺术馆，1996年。

人物山水笔搁
BRUSH HOLDER WITH MAN-IN-LANDSCAPE DESIGN

清（公元 1644～1911 年）
青玉
高 6.3、长 12.0 厘米

Qing (AD 1644 - 1911)
Green jade
Height, 6.3 cm; length, 12.0 cm

群峰耸立，峻石中有苍松一株，松下为持杖老者，旁侧为山间飞瀑。意境深远。

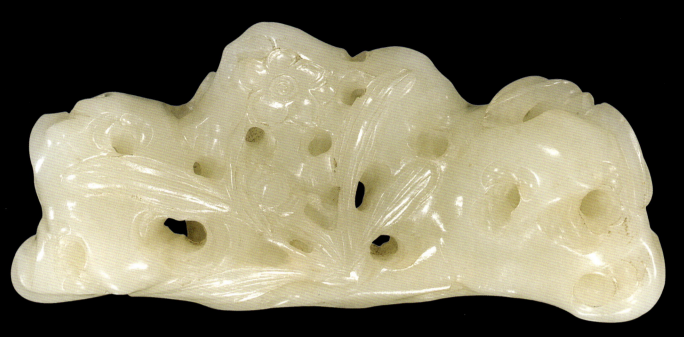

白玉花草笔搁
BRUSH HOLDER WITH FLOWER-AND-PLANT DESIGN

清（公元 1644～1911 年）
白玉 半透明
高 3.6、长 8.2 厘米

Qing (AD 1644 - 1911)
Translucent white jade
Height, 3.6 cm; length, 8.2 cm

条形湖石状。正背面分别刻有水仙、折技花草、瘦竹与灵芝。质地圆润，做工细腻，当为读书人心爱之物。

参见：

1.叶义《中国玉雕》图版 266，第 284、285 页。香港艺术馆，1983 年。
2.Watt,James,Chinese Jades From Han To Ching.(New York,The Asia Society,1980),NO.113.

鹅衔水草
GOOSE WITH WATER GRASS IN MOUTH

清（公元 1644～1911 年）
白玉 半透明
高 3.7、宽 4.0 厘米

Qing (AD 1644 - 1911)
Translucent white jade
Height, 3.7 cm; width, 4.0 cm

曲颈回首，敛翼团身，口衔一株长蔓水草，神态安逸恬淡，质地晶莹润泽。全器以整块卵形子玉雕成，做工精良，为乾隆时期坊间珍品佳作。

渔船
FISHING BOAT

清（公元 1644～1911 年）
青玉 半透明
高 5.5、长 16.0、宽 3.2 厘米

Qing (AD 1644 - 1911)
Translucent green jade
Height, 5.5 cm; length, 16.0 cm; width, 3.2 cm

船身前窄后宽，平底。船首系缆绳。船仓两侧为
透花活页窗棂。仓后置平顶凉棚，苫方格雨篷。船
舷一侧置铁首竹质长柄船蒿，一侧置竹质罟兜。仓
前甲板一侧蹲坐一头带斗笠的渔翁，渔翁一手扶
渔篓，一手探入篓内。仓顶平台上有两个围绕鱼
缸玩耍的小童，缸内有大鱼一条。凉棚下一人伏
身，手持扫帚探身刷洗船舷。另一人躬身直立，手
掌船舵。整器刻画细腻，制作精致。

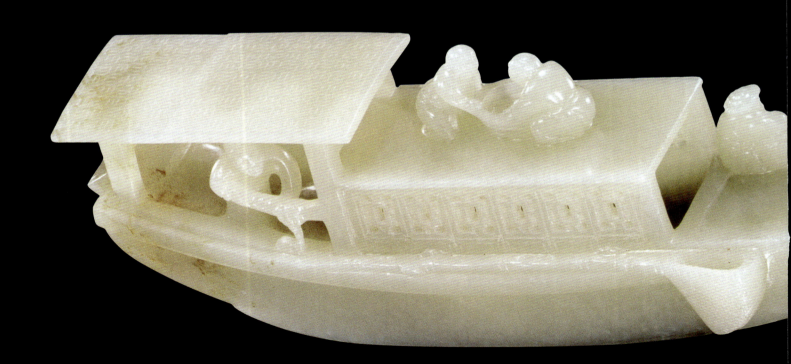

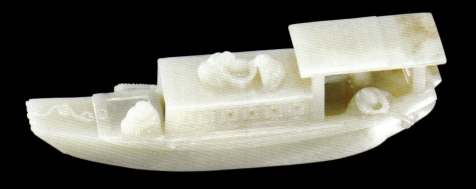

黄玉水丞
WATER CONTAINER

清（公元 1644～1911 年)
黄玉
高 3.1、口径 4.8、腹径 5.3 厘米

Qing (AD 1644 - 1911)
Yellow jade
Height, 3.1 cm; diameter, 4.8 cm (rim), 5.3 cm (belly)

敛口，圆形，由底部向器身饰涡旋状水波纹，此
类技法及造型常见于康乾时期。

参见：
叶义《中国玉雕》图版271、第288页。香港艺术馆，1983年。

白玉灵芝
LINGZHI-FUNGI

清（公元 1644～1911 年）
白玉 半透明
高 3.6、宽 4.5、厚 0.7 厘米

Qing (AD 1644 - 1911)
Translucent white jade
Height, 3.6 cm; width, 4.5 cm; thickness, 0.7 cm

灵芝三朵，为一大株二小株，其间有折技蔓草。全
器晶莹润泽，富有灵气。

白玉蝉纹香插
WORSHIPER'S VASE WITH CICADA DESIGN

清（公元 1644～1911 年）
白玉 半透明
高 11.3、宽 3.8 厘米

Qing (AD 1644 - 1911)
Translucent white jade
Height, 11.3 cm; width, 3.8 cm

长颈，扁平体，矮圈足。口部饰四朵云纹，颈下
与瓶体饰四组变形蝉纹。当为清乾隆朝仿青铜古
彝器而作，为佛堂陈设物，用于搁置小件上香用
具，故曰香插。

参见：
Watt，James，Chinese Jades From Han To Ching．(New York；The Asia
Society，1980)，NO．144．

黄玉福鼠佛手
BERGAMOT WITH BAT DESIGN

清（公元 1644～1911 年）
淡青黄玉 半透明
高 5.5、宽 2.8 厘米

Qing (AD 1644 - 1911)
Translucent light greenish-yellow jade
Height, 5.5 cm; width, 2.8 cm

底附蒂叶，上为佛手，叶间伏蝙蝠一只，寓意吉祥。

白玉 "子刚" 牌
PLAQUE WITH *ZI-GANG'S* INSCRIPTIONS

清（公元 1644～1911 年）
白玉 半透明
高 4.4、宽 3.1、厚 0.6 厘米

Qing (AD 1644 - 1911)
Translucent white jade
Height, 4.4 cm; width, 3.1 cm; thickness, 0.6 cm

长方玉牌。正面雕三国名将孙策，背刻"子刚"款
铭文。刻画细密传神，为康熙时期的玉作佳品。

参见：

1. 叶义《中国玉雕》，图版 261、第 282 页。香港艺术馆，1983 年。
2. 《玲珑玉雕》，图版 202A、第 225 页。香港大学美术博物馆，
1996 年。

少女晚妆牌
PLAQUE WITH LADY IN FRONT OF MIRROR

清（公元 1644～1911 年）
青白玉 半透明
高 4.7、宽 4.5、厚 0.8 厘米

Qing (AD 1644 - 1911)
Translucent pale green jade
Height, 4.7 cm; width, 4.5 cm; thickness, 0.8 cm

少女手持菱花临窗梳妆，背题"晚妆楼上杏花
浓"、"西湖勇"款。西湖勇，即冯勇，为乾隆朝
苏州玉作坊间高手，其作品传世者皆为精品。

参见：
《玲珑玉雕》，图版203A、第226页。香港大学美术博物馆，1996年。

御题诗牌
PLAQUE WITH EMPEROR'S POEM

清（公元 1644～1911 年）
青白玉　有褐斑
高 5.6、宽 3.6、厚 1.6 厘米

Qing (AD 1644 - 1911)
Pale green jade with brown patches
Height, 5.6 cm; width, 3.6 cm; thickness, 1.6 cm

正面饰花卉，背刻御题七律一首。为康乾时期作品。此器系用子玉制成，保留了卵石的原始形态。

参见：
《玲珑玉雕》，图版 3、第 27 页。香港大学美术博物馆，1996 年。

白玉鼻烟壶
SNUFF BOTTLE

清（公元 1644～1911 年）
白玉 半透明
高 6.0 厘米

Qing (AD 1644 - 1911)
Translucent white jade
Height, 6.0 cm

瓜棱形壶身，有盖。全器晶莹圆润，素洁高雅，当
为乾隆时期的宫廷用物。

参见：
《清朝瑰宝》，图版 251、第 385 页。香港艺术馆，1992 年。

俏色鼻烟壶
SNUFF BOTTLE

清（公元 1644～1911 年）
青白玉 有褐斑
高 7.0 厘米

Qing (AD 1644 - 1911)
Pale green jade with brown patches
Height, 7.0 cm

壶身圆润，有俏色，琥珀壶盖，小圈足。风格素净淡雅。

参见：
叶义《中国玉雕》，图版 217、第 242 页。香港艺术馆，1983 年。

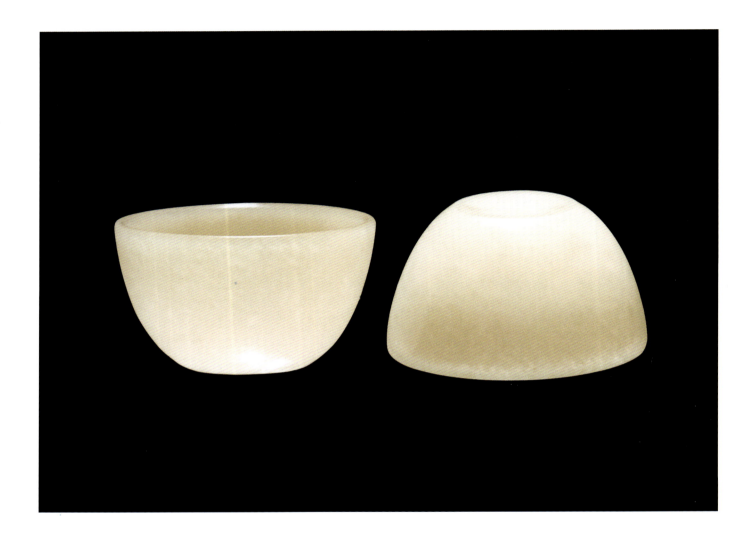

白玉双盏
PAIR OF BOWLS

清（公元1644～1911年）
白玉 半透明
高2.8、口径4.9厘米

Qing (AD 1644 - 1911)
Translucent white jade
Height, 2.8 cm; rim diameter, 4.9 cm

小巧玲珑，晶莹圆润，当为文人雅士品茗之物。平
底坡形内凹，当为清初之作。

"寿添海屋"扳指
RING WITH IMAGES OF IMMORTALITY

清（公元 1644～1911 年）
白玉　半透明
高 2.5、径 3.1 厘米

Qing (AD 1644 - 1911)
Translucent white jade
Height, 2.5 cm; diameter, 3.1 cm

丹墀海屋，飞鹤衔芝，题为"寿添海屋"。做工精细。

参见：
《玲珑玉雕》，图版207B、第230页。香港大学美术博物馆，1996年。

彩色图版目录
Color Photogragh Contents